ETHNIC CHRONOLOGY SERIES
NUMBER 6

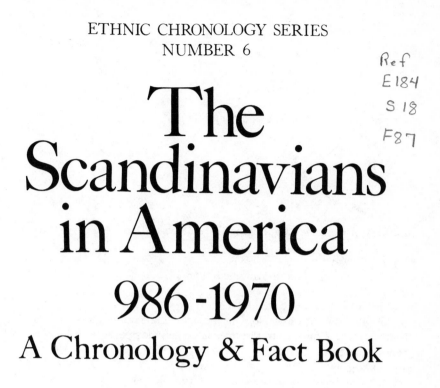

The Scandinavians in America

986-1970

A Chronology & Fact Book

Compiled and edited by

Howard B. Furer

1972
OCEANA PUBLICATIONS, INC.
DOBBS FERRY, NEW YORK

To Daddy

Who taught us to love life and each other.

Library of Congress Cataloging in Publication Data

Furer, Howard B   1934-
    The Scandinavians in America, 986-1970.

    (Ethnic chronology series, no. 6)
    SUMMARY: A chronology of the Scandinavians in the
United States from 986 to the present. Includes perti-
nent documents.
    Bibliography: p.
    1. Scandinavians in the United States--History.
[1. Scandinavians in the United States] I. Title.
II. Series.
E184.S18F87   917.3'06'395   72-10257
ISBN 0-379-00505-0

Manufactured in the United States of America

TABLE OF CONTENTS

EDITOR'S FOREWORD

The reader who is looking for a "Who's Who" of famous Scandinavian-Americans or a definitive treatment of Scandinavian immigration need go no further. The former has already been done several times, and the latter will have to wait until scholars produce the monographs upon which such a detailed study depends.

What is presented in this volume, space limitations aside, is a detailed chronology of pertinent facts concerning Scandinavians in America, a series of selected documents dealing with the subject, and a bibliography which can act as an excellent starting point for those students who are interested in pursuing further this vital area of American immigration history.

Because of the nature of Scandinavian immigration, a problem of integration was encountered, for Scandinavian immigration to the United States involved three distinct ethnic groups; the Danes, the Norwegians, and the Swedes. While every attempt was made to present these groups as an integrated whole, it became impossible to do so throughout the book. As a result, in essence, this is a volume which really contains three chronologies, and three bibliographies.

I have also sought to integrate the Scandinavian-American experience, as much as possible with some of the major themes in American history, realizing that the deeper significance of American immigration is lost if we try to tell the story of immigrants as a unique social occurrence.

Obviously, much more could have been included in this book, but again, space limitations caused the writer to be highly selective in his choice of key facts, pertinent documents and bibliography.

Finally, although the trend today among historians is to polarize the various ethnic groups which have come to make up American society, I am convinced that progress in immigration history will come, in the words of Oscar Handlin, "not by regarding it as the province of another group of subspecialists, but by seeing it in the context of the total American experience." It is time that immigrants are studied as the Americans they are.

Howard B. Furer
Newark State College.

SETTLEMENT IN THE 17TH AND 18TH CENTURIES

986-1003

The first known Scandinavian contacts with America may be credited to two Norwegians, Biarni Heriulfson, and Leif Ericsson, who, on separate voyages, reached the shores of America somewhere between Labrador and Cape Cod. Several later voyages failed to accomplish an intended colonization of "Vinland," the wooded, vine-covered shore which Leif Ericsson first explored. Recent research has uncovered some new information which tends to indicate that some of the Viking explorers may have penetrated the Americas as far west as Minnesota.

1004-1007

Thorvald Ericsson, Leif's brother explored the North American coast, using Leif's headquarters in Vinland.

1010-1013

Thorfinn Karlsevni, a trader from Iceland, with three ships and 160 men, sailed on an exploratory trip to the North American mainland. The possibility exists that Karlsevni, instead of coasting along Labrador or Newfoundland, sailed into Hudson's Bay.

1013

Karlsevni, it is believed, attempted to establish a colony at the western extremity of Long Island at a place he called "Straumsjord." His wife Gudrid bore a son there named Snoiri, the first white child born on the North American continent. However, Indian difficulties and other disturbances caused Karlsevni and his people to return home. Thus the first Norse attempt to colonize America failed, but voyages to Vinland apparently did not cease.

1630

May 24   The first Norwegian settlers to come to America arrived in the sheltered bay of New Amsterdam on a Dutch ship, de Eendracht. They were Roelof Jansen, his wife Anneke Jans, and her mother Tryn Jonas, all from Marstrand, Norway. They settled in with the Dutch settlers. Nor-

wegians were not the only representatives from the Scandinavian countries in the Dutch colony;   Danes were there
in even larger numbers, Swedes fewer.

1631

Several Norwegian families, led by Hugh Gunnison, settled
in New England. A few other Scandinavians, coming as
individual emigrants, came to America in the seventeenth
century.

1632

Tryn Jonas became the first midwife in New Netherland.
As the official midwife for the West India Company, she
was paid from public funds and was held in high honor by
the colonists for her service to the sick.

1633

A Norwegian ship carpenter, Hans Hansen Noorman came
to New Netherland with Wauter Von Twiller, the governor
of New Netherland. Noorman married a Dutch girl of
Walloon ancestry who bore him six children.

1634

From Bergen, Norway came Herman Hendricksen, the
progenitor of the Rosenkrans family in America, the most
distinguished decendent being General Willian S. Rosecrans,
Brigadier General of the Regular Army in the Civil War.

1638

March   A Swedish expedition, organized by William Usselinx, led
by Peter Minuit of Holland, and financed by the South Com-
pany of Sweden, arrived in America in the ship Kalmar
Nyckel.   The settlers established a Swedish colony called
Fort Christina, located at the present site of Wilmington,
Delaware.

1639

Although no statistics are available prior to 1820, we know
that some emigrants from Denmark had come to America,
and were active in the affairs of the colonies, and of the
new nation from the beginning.   Jones Bronck, for example,
came from the Danish Island of Funen to New Amsterdam in
1639, and gave his name to the borough of the Bronx in New
York City.

1640

April

The Swedish colony at Fort Christina survived its first two years with some difficulty. In the spring of 1640, the Swedish crown appointed Peter Rollender Ridder as governor, while the Reverend Reorus Torkillus, a Swedish Lutheran minister, some twenty-five new families, and much needed livestock arrived with this expedition.

Nov.

A group of Dutch settlers were planted 20 miles north of Fort Christina.

1643

The first Swedish clergyman to undertake conversion of the Indians to Christianity in the Delaware region was John Campanius. He wrote, in the language of the Lenapi Indians, the questions and answers in Luther's Little or Shorter Catechism.

Feb.

New Sweden received a new governor. He was Johan Bjornsson Printz, a Swedish soldier of fortune who led the colony from 1643 to 1653. He erected a series of blockhouses at Varkenskill, Upland, and Fort New Krisholm near the mouth of the Schuylkill (1647).

June

Printz established another settlement, New Gottenberg, about fifteen miles from Fort Christina. A few farmers took up land in the vicinity, but the settlements of New Sweden never included more than four hundred people or extended more than thirty-five miles along the Delaware River.

1643-1654

During this period, the Swedish settlers on the Delaware focused their main interest upon the fur trade. Farming was encouraged mainly as a means of support for the employees of the South Company. Governor Printz maintained good order and preserved friendly relations with the Indians. Lutheranism was designated as the official religion of the colony, although toleration was extended to Calvinists of the Dutch Reformed Church. It was also during these years that the Swedes erected the first log cabin in America.

1648

Apr. 27

Peter Stuyvesant built Fort Beversrede across the Delaware River to counteract Governor Printz's many Swedish establishments and blockhouses.

May   The Swedes burned and destroyed Fort Beversrede twice; once in May and again in November. Each time the Dutch rebuilt the fort, and posed a serious threat to the Swedish settlers in the small Delaware colony.

1654

Hugh Gunnison, the Norwegian immigrant in Boston, was made a deputy to the General Court of Massachusetts.

April   Johan Classon Rising replaced Printz as governor of New Sweden. He tried unsuccessfully to prevent the Dutch from penetrating the region occupied by the Swedes. The Dutch governor of New Amsterdam, Peter Stuyvesant, led repeated raids into New Sweden.

1654

June 8   Rising held a pow-wow with a dozen Indian chiefs. He distributed gifts among them, and the Indians promised additional tracts of land for the Swedes "as far as the Chesapeake."

1655

Sept. 26   Claiming the Delaware region as they did, the Dutch protested against Swedish occupation, although they did not seriously molest the Swedes for a number of years. In 1655, however, the Dutch sent an expedition of seven vessels which easily forced the surrender of Fort Christina, since the Dutch army was larger than the whole body of Swedish settlers. New Sweden became part of New Netherland, although the Swedes were permitted either to retain their lands or return to Sweden. Most of them stayed on and blended into the Dutch colony.

1656

March   A Swedish ship, the Mercurius, carrying more than a hundred Swedish settlers to New Sweden, arrived in front of Fort Casimir more than six months after the Swedish capitulation to the Dutch. They were not allowed to disembark. The leader of the group was Johan Papegoja, Governor Printz' son-in-law. Suddenly the ship lifted anchor, hoisted its sails, and sailed up the Delaware River to the former Swedish settlement of Tinicum, where the new colonists, much to the chagrin of the Dutch, disembarked. Faced with this fait-accompli, the Dutch allowed the Swedes to settle in this region under Dutch authority.

1660

In 1660, in the province of New Netherlands, two Norwegians, Laurens Andriessen and Laurens Laurensen, owned and operated two large sawmills. The Norwegians were particularly expert at sawing lumber.

1663

By 1663, the Swedes and Danes had 110 "boweries" (farms) in the Delaware area, with 200 cows, 20 horses, 80 sheep and several thousand pigs.

From time to time, single settlers or even groups of Swedes arrived in America; sixty emigrants arrived at New Amsterdam. Some of these were Finns, who at that time were Swedish subjects.

1664

Sept. 7   Dutch New Amsterdam was conquered by an English fleet commanded by Colonel Richard Nicolls. The colony was renamed New York, in honor of its proprietor, James, Duke of York, and the Swedish settlers now found themselves under English rule.

1674

Emigration from Norway to New York did not entirely cease, but from 1674 on, there was a marked decrease, mainly because Norway discovered through her connection with Holland that she, too, had a future on the sea, and instead of sending her youth to help man foreign fleets she now employed them in building up her own.

1683

A year after William Penn arrived in his new colony of Pennsylvania, which included the lands that had formerly belonged to New Sweden, one hundred and eighty eight families on both sides of the Delaware River, comprising nine hundred and twenty four persons were listed as Swedish.

1688

May   Reverend Lars Karlsson Lock, the only remaining Swedish clergyman from the original New Sweden colony died. This left the Swedish settlers without the benefit of Swedish Lutheran clergy for many years.

1691

Andrew Printz, a nephew of the former governor of New
Sweden visited the Swedish settlers in Pennsylvania. He
was primarily concerned with meeting their religious
needs, and subsequently arranged, with the help of King
Charles XI of Sweden, to send both new prayer books and
ministers to the Swedish settlers.

1693

Because of a lack of Swedish Lutheran pastors in America,
nearly 1,000 individuals signed an appeal to the Swedish
crown for Swedish pastors.   Four years passed before any
action was taken.

1697

There were 1,200 people in Delaware who spoke Swedish by
1697.

June 24   Andreas Rudman, Erik Bjorck, and Jonas Auren, three
young divinity students from Uppasala, Sweden, arrived in
America to provide religious leadership for the Swedes on
the Delaware.   They built new churches and parsonages.

1699

June 4   The first permanent Swedish Lutheran church in America
was dedicated at Cranebrook, Delaware. It was called
the Trinity, a name it still bears.

1700

A Swedish church, Gloria Dei, was dedicated in Philadelphia.   It is the oldest church building now standing in
Philadelphia, and since 1943 it has been an official American national monument.

1702

The first full book about America was printed in Stockholm.   It was called A Short Description of the Province
of New Sweden, and was written by Johan Campanius Holm,
a grandson of the Reverend Johan Campanius who had translated the catechism for the Indians.

1711

Gustavus Hesselius, a Swedish immigrant, began his
career as an artist in Delaware and Maryland.

1730

By 1730, the descendents of the original Swedish settlers were being rapidly Anglicized. One Swedish preacher felt obliged to hold three vesper services: one in German, one in English, and one in Swedish.

1740

Sept.

When the German Moravian colonists founded their colonies at Bethlehem, Pennsylvania, there were among them several Norwegian emigrants. Jost Jensen was an innkeeper there, and between sixty and seventy Norwegian names have been identified in the old Moravian churchyard.

1750

Requests were coming from the old Swedish settlements of Delaware and Pennsylvania for church services to be conducted entirely in English.

1753

June

Another group of Norwegians settled at a second Moravian colony at Bethabara, North Carolina. Hans Martin Kalberlahn of Trondhjem, Norway was among them, and became one of the first bonafide physicians in the colonies.

1754

Most of the descendants of the original Swedish colonists of the seventeenth century had, by this time, intermarried with the other nationalities in the colonies. Although these Swedes had lost most of their old country traits, more than nine hundred of them still spoke their native tongue.

1758

The most famous of the Swedish pastors of the eighteenth century in America was Reverend Israel Acrelius who deplored the lessening of religious zeal and the extravagances of the younger generation.

1769

A Society of Scandinavians was founded in Philadelphia as a socio-cultural organization.

1770

By 1770, all the descendents of the original Swedish settlers on the Delaware were catechized in English exclusively.

1774

Occassionally individual Swedes emigrated to the American colonies. Some went on to become quite prominent. Among the mid-eighteenth century arrivals were Ulric Wertmuller, a noted portrait painter (1794), John Asplund, a preacher (1784), Carl Frederick Arensburg, an outstanding judge and civic leader, (1721), and Colonel John Christian Senf, an engineer who came to South Carolina, later fought in the Revolutionary War, and in the 1790's built the Santee Canal in South Carolina, one of the earliest in the United States.

1776

July 2   John Morton of Delaware, a descendant of one of the early Swedish settlers, cast the deciding vote in favor of the Declaration of Independence.

Dec. 24   Although documentary proof is lacking, most sources indicate that the Swedes, living along the Delaware River were probably among the farmers who rowed George Washington and his men across the rapids for his surprise attack on the English and Hessians.

Four out of five Norwegian seamen are known to have enlisted as soldiers in the colonial army in New York.

1776-1781

The Swedes along the Delaware were subjected to great hardships and untold suffering by the English troops because of their loyalty to the Revolutionary cause. They fought in large numbers in the ranks, and they furnished some of the most brilliant officers and leaders in the struggle.

1779

By 1779, forty-one Swedish pastors had been sent to America to tend to the spiritual and moral needs of the Swedes still living along the Delaware.

Sept. 23 Two Norwegian seamen, Thomas Johnson, and Lars Bruun of Mandal, Norway, served under Captain John Paul Jones, taking part in the battle between the Bonhomme Richard and the Serapis.

1780

By this time, practically all contacts with Sweden by Swedish colonists in America had been allowed to lapse, and because so many Swedish names had been changed in spelling or otherwise corrupted, these Swedish Americans are often hard to identify.

1781

Nov. 5 John Hanson, another descendant of the early Swedish pioneers, was elected President of the Congress under the Articles of Confederation government. He served in that capacity until 1787.

1787

The last Swedish minister returned to Sweden. Many of the descendants of the colonial Swedes, by this time, had been absorbed into the Episcopalian church.

Sept. 17 As a group, the Scandinavians in the United States strongly supported the framing of the Constitution, and John Hanson performed valuable service in working for its final ratification.

1789

June 25 Jurisdiction over the "Old Swedes" churches in the United States was transferred by the Archbishop of Sweden, Uno von Troil, to the American Protestant Episcopal Church, which still exercises control.

1793

July 25 Individual emigrants from the Scandinavian countries continued to come to the United States although the numbers were very small as a result of the French Revolutionary wars. One of those who did leave Europe was a Swede from Stockholm named Jacob Fahlstrom. He became an expert woodsman and fur trapper, and was the first known Swede to settle in Minnesota. In time, he bought a farm at Afton, Minnesota where he died in 1857.

1799

L. A. Iverson, a Norwegian sea captain settled in Georgia.
The family remained, and an Iverson, one of the Captain's
grandsons, became United States Senator from Georgia in
the years preceding the Civil War.

SETTLEMENT IN THE NINETEENTH CENTURY (1800-1860)

1805

Torgus Torkelsen Gromstu, a seaman from Ajerpen, Norway, settled in New York in the spring of 1805.

1814

April   The Napoleonic Wars further constricted Scandinavian
emigration to the United States.   However, an occassional
emigrant from the Norse Countries did make the journey.
One of the most prominent was Raphael Widen from Sweden.
After having established a successful business in New York,
he became the first known Swede to settle in Illinois.   He
achieved some prominence in local Illinois politics, and like
most Swedes he was a strong opponent of slavery.   In 1824,
Widen helped to pass a law which banned slavery from Illinois.   However, Widen kept up no contacts with other Swedish settlers and made no attempts to promote Swedish
immigration to Illinois.

1821

Aug.   Cleng Peerson, the Norwegian "pathfinder in the West,"
and Knud Olsen Eide journeyed from Stavanger, Norway to
New York by way of Goteborg.   Both men were probably
sent to the United States as the agents of a group of Quakers in Stavanger who desired to find a place of refuge where
they might worship God as they pleased.

1824

May   Peerson returned to Norway, and reported to his friends
about the conditions and prospects for immigrants in the
United States.   During the summer of 1824, the group of
Norwegian Quakers in and about Stavanger determined to
emigrate.

1824

Sept.   Peerson returned to the United States to begin preparations
for the coming of the first group of Norwegian emigrants.

1825

April   Peerson purchased six pieces of land from Joseph Fellows,
                         the agent of the Pultney Land Office, which had control of a
                         large amount of land in Western New York State.

Oct. 9   A group of fifty-three Norwegians arrived in New York City
                         aboard the ship Restauration.   The "sloop party," as they
                         were known, were greeted by Cleng Peerson.

Oct. 19   The "sloop party," led by Peerson, left New York City and
                         made their way to upper New York State passing through
                         Albany on October 22.

Oct. 31   The fifty-three Norwegians arrived at the site chosen by
                         Peerson, several years earlier.   It was located near Ro-
                         chester, New York.   The settlers called their colony Ken-
                         dall Settlement.   Each adult male of the group purchased
                         a tract of forty acres at $5 an acre from the Pultney Land
                         agent.   However, after this first influx, there was no fur-
                         ther planned Norwegian immigration for more than a de-
                         cade, and it was not until the 1840's that the movement
                         really began to gather momentum, as a result of religious
                         and economic factors in Norway.

1825-1836

Information concerning America began to be transmitted
back to Norway in letters from those immigrants who had
already settled in the new world.   These documents were
called "America Letters," and were important in inducing
additional Scandinavian groups to emigrate.   After 1836,
the volume of letters increased.

1826

Beginning in 1826 and continuing until 1910, Norway gave
to America a larger proportion of her people than any
other nation, except Ireland, during the great Atlantic migrations.

The first Norwegians to settle in the mid-west experienced
both joys and suffering.   His original dwelling was a sod
hut, built up against a slope, with two or three steps to go
down before reaching the dirt floor.   The room was seldom
more than twelve feet long, fourteen feet wide, and eight
feet high.   Daylight had to come in through the door, and
smoke go out through a hole in the dirt roof.

1828

July 24   One of the "sloop party," Ole Johnson, returned to Stav-
            anger, was married there to a member of the Quaker
            Society, and very soon thereafter again departed for Amer-
            ica. He convinced several members of his family to
            accompany him.

1829-1832

Several Norwegians made individual emigrant ventures to
the United States during these years. Most of them were
from southwestern Norway, but Johan Nordboc came from
eastern Norway in 1832, and thus was one of the earliest
emigrants from an area that was later to contribute large
numbers to the movement. Most of the new emigrants,
including Nordboc, went to the Kendall Settlement.

1831

Gjert Hovland, from the district of Hardanger, north of
Stavanger, came to America. Copies of his enthusiastic
letters were widely circulated through his home district,
inspiring many other people to emigrate to the new world.

1833

March   Cleng Peerson set out on an exploratory journey to the
            west in search of suitable lands for settlement by Norweg-
            ians. He finally selected a site in Illinois in the Fox
            River region of La Salle County.

1834

The Kendall Settlement had grown to fourteen families,
and they changed the name of their colony to Ellenaais.

May   Six families from the Kendall Settlement moved to Illin-
            ois and established a second Norwegian settlement in the
            United States.....the "Fox River Settlement."

1835

June   The six Norwegian families bought land in La Salle County
            for $1.25 an acre, although they had staked out their claims
            in May of the previous year.

July   Several other families from Kendall moved to Illinois.
            They were led by Nels Nelson Hersdahl, and Gjert G.
            Hovland.

1836

Probably the first two Norwegians to settle permanently in Chicago were Halstein Torrison with his family, and Johan Larson, a sailor.

Among the earliest nineteenth century Swedish settlers shipwrecked or had deserted in some American port. The first known of this type of emigrant was Svante Magnus Svensson who was shipwrecked off the coast of Galveston, Texas. He remained in Texas, and later amassed a fortune in cattle, cotton, and banking.

The Swedish Society, which still exists, was founded in New York City, with the purpose of performing charitable services for incoming Swedish emigrants. No religious services were provided at first.

May 25   A Norwegian emigrant vessel, the Norden, with 110 passengers left Stavanger for New York. Knud Anderson Slogvig was the leader of this group, and we may say that large scale emigration from Norway had begun. Contemporary writers often attributed the exodus to religious discontent; it is a fact that many immigrants sympathized with the pietistic movement known as Haugeanism in its struggle with the state church, and some of them were members of minor dissenting sects such as Quakers. But the underlying causes of emigration were primarily economic; rapidly increasing population and lands being subdivided until holdings became too small to support those who cultivated them. Under these circumstances, a large proportion of Norwegian emigrants consisted of bonders, or freeholders who saw in emigration the only alternative to a drop in status. The movement also drew in its wake both husmond (cotters), laborers, and servants.

June 8   The Den Norske Klippe, with 57 Norwegians left Stavanger for New York. In addition there were some who went by sloop to Goteborg, where they got passage for New York. All told, the emigration of 1836 was in the vicinity of 200 persons.

Sept.   By the fall of 1836, most of the Norwegian immigrants had reached the mid-West. The Fox River Settlement was thriving and some persons had settled in Chicago. The Kendall Settlement had practically run its course.

1837

April 7   The Aegir sailed from Bergen, Norway with 84 emigrants and during the following months several other ships left for America. All told, there were 215 Norwegians in these groups. Upon arrival in the United States, they all headed for Illinois and the Fox River Settlement. Ole Rynning became the leader of this large party.

May

Cleng Peerson was engaged by a group of dissatisfied Norwegian immigrants from Fox River to search out a new place for settlement. He selected a spot in northeastern, Missouri in Shelby County. A party of 12 or 14 Norwegians, led by Knud Slogvig and Sjur J. Haseim, left Fox River and proceeded to this new site, a place located 25 miles from Shelbyville, Missouri. Claims were taken, and log houses built, but the immigrants had a difficult time. Haaeim, after one year's trial, gave up and returned to Norway. Peerson, Slogvig and the others stayed on.

May 22

A party of more than 50 Norwegians started from Tind, Telemarken for America via Göteborg. They were organized so that they could give mutual aid to one another.

Aug.

The group headed by Ole Rynning, after hearing some unfavorable reports about the Fox River Settlement, changed their direction, and went to Beaver Creek, some 70 miles south of Chicago in Iroquois County, where they selected land and built their log houses. However, the settlement at Beaver Creek was a bad mistake. The land was poor and marshy, while a severe epidemic of typhoid fever invaded the colony and claimed lives daily.

Aug. 7

A severe economic panic struck the United States, and like many other Americans, the Scandinavian immigrants were adversely affected. A report of the Swedish-Norwegian Vice-Consul in New York, A. Zacharison, stated that Swedes and Norwegians should not emigrate to the United States because of the adverse economic conditions. This advice seems to have had very little effect in Scandinavia.

1838

Exhortations in letters and on the tongues of returned travelers began to be augmented by the printed word. The most influential was Ole Rynning's True Account of America. Many Norwegians began their first lessons in reading with it.

Occassionally, a well-to-do immigrant aided poor Norwegians to emigrate. Ole Aasland, a rich farmer from Flesberg, Numedal, took a group of poor emigrants with him to America, on the condition that they would repay him in labor. From Kendall, New York, he proceeded to Noble

County, Indiana, where he bought a large tract of land. However, the sickness and deaths of a considerable number of his associates defeated his plan, and he later exchanged his Indiana lands for a small tract close to the Kendall Settlement. A few of the emigrants stayed on in Indiana, however, forming the first Scandinavian contingent in that state.

1838

March

Cleng Peerson came to New York City to recruit newly arriving Norwegian emigrants for his Missouri colony. He persuaded one group led by Peter and William Testman to accompany him west. The party initially numbered 22 persons, and while some went to Chicago, the majority settled in Shelby County, Missouri. Several other settlers were added to this colony in 1839, but on the whole the settlement was unsuccessful, and after a few years it began to disintegrate. The fact that Missouri was a slave state made it unattractive to Norwegian immigrants, while Norwegians tended to follow the crowd which was beginning to flock to the fertile unoccupied lands of Wisconsin.

April

Most of the Beaver Creek's settlers moved back to Fox River in La Salle County. The last to leave was Mons Aadland, who in 1840 exchanged his farm for a small herd of cattle and went to Wisconsin.

July 1

Ole Nattestad left the Beaver Creek Colony and went to, what is now, Clinton Township, Rock County, Wisconsin. He laid out a claim, built a log house, and became the founder of an important Wisconsin settlement of Norwegians----the Jefferson Prairie Settlement. Thousands upon thousands were to follow his footsteps several years later.

Aug.

Gullick O. Gravdal and Gisle S. Hallan, two immigrants not content with the location of the Jefferson Prairie site, founded the Rock Prairie Settlement west of the city of Beloit, Wisconsin.

1839

The Norwegian emigration of 1839 was twice as large as that of 1837. There would be a decline in 1840, but in 1841, the number would equal that of 1839, and during 1842 it would nearly double.

May

Sixty Norwegians under the leadership of John Nelson Luraas arrived in Boston. Their original plan was to go to Fox River, but they went instead to Muskego Lake, Waukesha County, Wisconsin, where they established a settlement. It became the best known Norwegian settlement in America, and in time, expanded into Norway Township and several adjoining townships in Racine County.

June The main emigrant party of Ole Nattestad's Jefferson Prairie Settlement assembled at Drammen, Norway. They were led by Ole's brother Ansten Nattestad. Between 130 to 140 people embarked for America on the ship Emilia. After arriving in New York City they followed the now familiar route west, stopping at Kendall to consult with the wealthiest Norwegian immigrant in that region, Lars Larsen.

1839

September Ansten Nattestad's party arrived at the Jefferson Prairie Settlement where they were met by Ole Nattestad. The new settlers purchased tracts of land, and began farming procedures almost immediately.

1840

Sweden's Immigration Law of 1768 restricting the right of emigration was repealed by the Swedish parliament, primarily because of the need to meet the growing problem of pauperism in Sweden. As a result, the floodgates of Swedish emigration to the United States were about to open.

Emigrant companies, such as the American Emigrant Company, the Columbia Emigrant Company and others, advertised in the Swedish press as semi philanthropic enterprises to protect immigrants from their unscrupulous countrymen; and some of them actually did good work by having their employees meet newcomers on arrival, providing them with interpreters and clean boarding houses, and maintaining an employment department.

May The first Swedes arrived in Chicago, and seventeen of them decided to settle there permanently. To this city's development, the chief contributions of the Swedes would be as builders, whether as architects, contractors, or carpenters.

June Norwegians began moving into Iowa. The first Norwegian settlement there was the Sugar Creek colony in Lee County, founded by Hans Barlien. However, heavy

1840

Norwegian movement into Iowa did not occur until after 1849 when immigrants began to spill out into northeastern Iowa from the heavily concentrated Wisconsin settlements.

July

Only six years after the original Norwegian settlement in Illinois had been established, Norwegians were moving into Wisconsin by two approaches, the Lake Michigan shore and the Illinois boundary.

July 14

Several other Norwegian settlements, offshoots of the Ole Nattestad colony, were founded. They included a settlement in Illinois, partly in Stephenson County, and partly in Winnebago County under the leadership of Clement Torstenson Staback; and a settlement at Wind Lake founded by Soren Bache and Johannes Johansen.

August

Even Heg, the leader of a group of Norwegian immigrants arrived at the Muskego Settlement in Wisconsin. Soon Heg became the head of this prosperous colony. He purchased the farm of John Nelson Luraas, the original founder and Heg's home became the mecca for hundreds of Norwegians in search of homes in Wisconsin and the west.

September

One of the most important of the Wisconsin settlements, and certainly the most prosperous was the Koshkonong Settlement, taking its name from Koshkonong Creek and Lake, and having its nucleus in the southeastern portion of Dane County, the southwestern part of Jefferson County, and the northern part of Rock County. After the initial settlements had been made, waves of new immigrants moved into a second Dane County area. Settlements soon overflowed into Columbia County and others, and as time passed Koshkonong Settlement became a kind of mother colony to numerous settlements in Wisconsin and other parts of the mid-west.

October

By the fall, several of the 1839 Jefferson Prairie immigrants had taken up land at the Rock Prairie Settlement. Among them were Lars H. Skavlem, Gjermund Skavlem, and Knud Christbinusen. In the following years, this settlement grew by leaps and bounds, especially after 1843, and became a starting point for immigrants pushing further into the interior.

1840-1843

A significant rise in Norwegian emigration to the United States occurred during these years. The official figures

1840-1843

are 300 emigrants in 1840, 400 in 1841, 700 in 1842 and 1600 in 1843.

1841

Many a Scandinavian immigrant was fleeced in New York or Chicago by unscrupulous immigrant "runners" who sold him bogus tickets or land claims to which they had no title.

As the dissemination of Norwegian immigrants proceeded in the early 1840's, a number of small settlements sprang up upon a purely individual basis.   The lead mines in Lafayette County, Wisconsin attracted a number of immigrants, as well as the mines in the adjacent Illinois County, Jo Davies.

May 11   Gustaf Unonius, his wife, and three of his university friends, Ivor Hagberg, Carl Groth, and William Palman, left Galve, Sweden for settlement in America.   Arriving in New York City, Unonius was advised by a fellow countryman, A. Brodell, to try his luck in northern Illinois.

May 18   The Unonius party set out by boat, via the Erie Canal, for Illinois, but on board the vessel they heard that the best land in Illinois had already been taken.   Unonius met other immigrants on board the canal boat, and as a majority of his new friends debarked at Milwaukee, the Unonius party decided to get off there too.

1841

July   Unonius met Olof Gottfried Lange, the only Swede then living in Milwaukee.   Lange agreed to act as guide to this immigrant party in their search for available land.

November 11 Unonius purchased 160 acres of land on a little lake near Delafield, Wisconsin, on the road to Madison, known as Pine Lake.   The Swedes named their colony New Uppsala, and built their log houses which were finished happily by Christmas time.

1842

April   The Pine Lake colony received an influx of a motley collection of newly arrived Swedes, the majority of whom were serious-minded farm workers.   This colony, in general, was never really successful.

Peter Cassel was the founder of the first Swedish settlement

1842

in Iowa, when he arrived in 1842 to found New Sweden in Jefferson County, the first permanent nineteenth century settlement by Swedes.

August 8   Emigration interest was flaming in Telemarken and Numedal, Norway especially.   One hundred and seventy six Norwegian emigrants arrived in New York aboard the bark Ellida.   It had been a voyage of misery.   Nine passengers had died from cholera or typhus, and thirty others were transferred from the ship to a New York hospital.   The immigrants of 1842 seemed to have been, in general, very poor, and their poverty added greatly to the economic difficulties of the settlers in the west, upon whose hospitality they were thrown.

October 25   One of the emigrant ships of 1842 brought back to Norway an emigrant whose narrative of American experiences was given wide publicity.   He was Knud Aslaksen Svalestuen, a Telemarken "bønde" who had emigrated in 1839, and whose stories excited emigration fever once more.

1843

Gustaf Flack, a Swedish ex-sailor from Victoria, Illinois, was instrumental in inducing, by his letters, the first planned group of Swedish settlers to Illinois.

The Even Heg barn at Muskego was used as a sort of a boarding house for new immigrants.   Sunday school classes were held in it, and in 1844 the Reverend C. L. Clausen confirmed the first group of Norwegian children there.

1843

Maximilian Scheele De Vere, who came to the United States from Sweden in 1843, was one of the founders of the American Philosophical Society.

A curious pioneer institution in early Scandinavian communities was the bathhouse, which was the sauna of the nineteenth century.   It was first introduced by the Swedes at Pine Lake, Wisconsin in 1843.

The total of Scandinavian emigrants to the United States in this year reached well over 1800.

The Swedish-Norwegian government appointed a commission to investigate emigration from Norway to the United

1843

States, and to consider regulatory measures.

March   The Danish publisher, Laurite Fribert, wrote a roseate
                 description of conditions in Wisconsin which induced bands
                 of Danes to emigrate.

April 27   Cleng Peerson returned to Norway to stir up emigration
                 interest. His verbal accounts, favorable "America Let-
                 ters," and economic distress prompted a comparatively
                 large emigration during the summer of 1843. Nine emi-
                 grant vessels sailed from Norwegian ports for New York
                 and seven from La Havre, France. Peerson, himself,
                 returned to America in June, 1843.

                 The celebrated Concord, Massachusetts feminist and au-
                 thor, Margaret Fuller, together with her friend Sara Free-
                 man Clarke visited the Swedish settlement at Pine Lake,
                 Wisconsin.

October   Hans Gasmann, and several other Norwegian immigrants
                 joined the Swedish colony at Pine Lake.

December   Ole Valle and Ole Tollefson Kittilsland began the Swedish
                 migration to Iowa. Larger migrations would take place
                 in 1849-1850.

1844

The United States government sent the reports of its land
office to American consuls in Sweden, to be made available there in Swedish translations, but many immigrants
did not have the foresight to consult such official agencies.

S. M. Svensson, who had settled in Texas in 1836, organized
a permanent Swedish colony around the city of Austin,
Texas.

March   A religious colonizer in Wisconsin, who attracted numer-
                 ous new immigrants was the Danish pioneer minister, C. L.
                 Clausen. He did excellent work not only among the scatter-
                 ed Danish immigrants, but also among Norwegian settlers.
                 In the late 1840's, Reverend Clausen was visited at the Rock
                 Prairie Settlement in Wisconsin by the famous Norwegian
                 jurist Ole Munch Raeder.

1844

April   A considerable emigration from Sogn, Norway took place, and some of the emigrants from this district took the lead in founding an Illinois settlement known as Long Prairie.

J. W. C. Dietrichson, a Norwegian Lutheran minister, arrived in Koshkonong, and proceeded to organize a number of Lutheran congregations in Wisconsin so as to prevent Norwegian-Americans from straying from the established church in the homeland. Dietrichson, later joined by the Reverend Hans A. Stub, laid the foundations for the Norwegian Lutheran Church institutions in the United States.

1845

Lars Larsen, one of the original members of the "sloop party" who had settled in Rochester, New York with his wife Martha and his daughter Margaret Allen, lost his life in a canal boat accident.

A large emigration from Sogn, Norway began, and although some of these immigrants went to Chicago, the majority joined the Long Prairie Settlement in Illinois which had been established the previous year by emigrants from the same district in Norway. A small splinter group, led by Ole Olsen Menes, settled at Koshkonong.

Svante Palm, a former Swedish journalist, and the uncle of S. M. Svensson emigrated to Texas. He was the first educated Swede to arrive there, and in 1846 when Texas had been annexed to the United States, he was appointed postmaster of the town of La Grange, Texas.

By 1845, most Norwegian emigration was coming from two general areas----the coastal region embracing the three counties on the southwest, and the south-central counties, mainly Bratsberg and Buskerud. The areas outside of these regions were almost untouched.

January 6   Eighty Norwegians of the Muskego Settlement attached their names to an open letter addressed to the people of Norway in which they praised America, and denounced any and all anti-emigration writings in Norway.

January   Johan Reierson, a Norwegian who had originally settled in Wisconsin, and a great defender of emigration, formally announced his intention to lead a party of emigrants to New Orleans, and those who were interested were invited to enroll.

1845

April 25   Peter Cassel led a group of Swedish emigrants to Iowa.
              There he established the first Swedish colony in Iowa,
              appropriately called New Sweden. Their guide had been
              Peter Dahlberg, who had come to America in 1843, and
              who had roamed as far west as Wisconsin, Iowa and Min-
              nesota.

May   The first Norwegian-Lutheran Church in America was
              built at Muskego with a gift of $400 from Tallef Bache of
              Drammen, Norway.

May 25   The most potent agents in directing the early Swedish mi-
              grants to Illinois were two Methodist ministers of Swedish
              birth, the brothers Olaf Gustaf and Jonas J. Hedström, the
              former stationed in New York as an American Methodist
              missionary to Scandinavian sailors and immigrants, and
              the other working at Victoria, Illinois. Olaf began preach-
              ing to the incoming Swedish emigrants on board the Bethel
              Ship moored at Pier 11 on the Hudson River on behalf of
              the Methodist Church. In addition to spiritual matters, he
              advised them to go to Illinois.

June   The Johan Reierson party arrived in New Orleans, and
              then proceeded to Texas where they established a settle-
              ment named "Normandy" at Brownsboro in northeastern
              Texas. However, very few additional immigrants chose
              to go to the Reierson colony.

July   Reierson returned to Norway, and established a magazine
              called Norge og Amerike. It served as a convenient ve-
              hicle for the publication of "America Letters," as well
              as Reierson's own writings which promoted emigration.
              Shortly thereafter, he returned to his Texas colony.

November   Olof Olsson met Olaf Hedström at the Bethel Ship in New
              York. He had come as a representative of Eric Janson,
              leader of a Swedish religious sect known as the Jansonites,
              frowned upon by the Swedish government. His mission was
              to scout for land in America, and Hedström again suggested
              Illinois.

1846

Norwegian emigrants paid $25 to $38 for a ticket to the
United States from Norway, the immigrant furnishing his
own food and bedding.

A Guide to Self-Instruction in the English Language was
published at Bergen, Norway as an aid to prospective emigrants.

1846

March   Ole Valle and Ole Tollefson Kittilsland, who had come, to
                Iowa in 1843, established a Norwegian settlement in Clay-
                ton County.

May   "America Letters" sent back to Sweden by Peter Cassel
                caused two additional groups to leave Kisa for the New
                Sweden colony in Iowa. The first group, consisting of
                42 persons, headed for New Sweden but lost their way
                and wound up near present day Des Moines. This area
                was then Indian country with only a few white settlers.
                By the end of September, 1846, they had recrossed half
                the state of Iowa, and finally reached New Sweden.

                When war was declared on Mexico, Scandinavian immi-
                grants, displaying a characteristic patriotism, volunteered
                for the army in relatively large numbers, and fought with
                distinction in a number of major engagements.

June   Eric Janson, leader of the Swedish pietistic sect known as
                Jansonites, arrived in New York where he was met by Olaf
                Olsson and Olaf Hedström. They laid plans to go west.

August   Fifty Norwegian emigrants made their way to Texas, and
                during the following year about 30 more arrived at the
                "Normandy" Settlement. The most influential of this group
                was Elise Amalie Warrenskjold, who became an inportant
                contributor to Reiersen's magazine.

August 1   Olaf Olsson left Eric Janson in New York and went west. He
                took title to 60 acres of new land near Red Oak Grove of
                Henry County, Illinois, the price being $250.

August 21   Janson arrived in Illinois, and he and Olsson purchased a
                complete farm of 156 acres with buildings and livestock
                for $1,100. At this farm, both the Olsson and Janson fami-
                lies lived while they prepared for the arrival of their fol-
                lowers from Sweden.

September 26   Olsson and Janson bought 480 acres of government land at
                the prevailing price of $1.25 an acre. These purchases in-
                cluded Hoopal Grove, the center of "Bishop Hill," the name
                Janson gave to his new settlement in Illinois.

October   Four families of the New Sweden "lost party" liked the un-
                populated region they had stumbled upon by accident, and
                they decided to stay. They called their tiny settlement
                Swede Point, which was later known as Madrid, Iowa.

1846

December 31   According to a Swedish-Norwegian consular report, 502
Norwegian and 910 Swedish sailors had deserted their
ships to remain as settlers in the United States.

1847

The first Danish settlement in Wisconsin was made in
Waukesha County, not far from the growing city of Milwaukee.

S. M. Svensson induced Swedish land workers as well as
members of his own family to move to his colony in Texas.
His sister Ana became the first Swedish born woman to
enter Texas, and the entire party numbered 25 persons.

January   The first Scandinavian newspaper in the United States was
established at New York City.   This paper, Skandinavia,
with Christian Hansen as one of its promoters, was intended
to serve the needs of Danes, Norwegians and Swedes.

February   Beginning in the winter of 1847 and continuing until June,
1854, nine different groups, adding up to almost 1,500 persons arrived at "Bishop Hill" colony from Sweden. Such
numbers testified to the power exercised by Eric Janson.
The "Biship Hill" colony contributes an interesting chapter
to the history of communal societies in the United States.

April 15   The first Scandinavian reading room in the United States
was opened in New York City.

April 22   A hundred emigrants from Toten, Modurm, and Telemarken, Norway settled at Koshkonong.   Good land and the
spirit of adventure seems to have brought this group to
this colony.

Ole Münch Raeder, a prominent lawyer and jurist from
Norway, was sent to the United States to study the operations of the American jury system. He sent home regular
dispatches, for newspaper publication, concerned with the
Norwegian immigration communities in the United States.
His work was an unconscious form of propaganda motivating many Norwegians to go to America.

June 29   The first Norwegian-American Newspaper was established
at Muskego, Wisconsin. It was called Nordlyset (Northern
Lights), and was published by J. D. Reymert. It remained
in existence until 1849, and championed the Free Soil
Party.

July   The Norwegian-Swedish Consul General, Adam Løvensk-
                jold, visited the Norwegian and Swedish Settlements in
                Wisconsin, and wrote a lively report about the thriving
                settlements in that state which was officially presented to
                the governments on October 15, 1847.

Sept. 16   Thomas and Kari Veblen, the parents of the renowned Nor-
                wegian-American social scientist, Thorstein Veblen, ar-
                rived in Milwaukee. Thorstein was born in Manitowac
                County, Wisconsin.

                                    1847

Oct. 15   Adam Lovenskjold reported that, in general, Norwegians
                were not taking part in American politics, and because of
                their "General ignorance" they were being called "Norweg-
                ian Indians" by the native Americans.

                                    1848

                Targe G. Mandt, who came with his parents from Tele-
                marken, Norway, to Dane County, Wisconsin, was the
                creator of the "Staughton Wagon" used by thousands of
                farmers in the northwest during the last three decades of
                the nineteenth century. It was often called the perfect farm
                wagon.

                Over 4,000 "America Letters" were sent back to Norway,
                and went from parish to parish, sometimes hundreds of
                copies of an original letter finding their way into widely
                dispersed homes. They spoke of the ease of acquiring
                land.

                A Swedish Lutheran congregation was established at New
                Sweden colony in Iowa.

January   The first Swedish-Lutheran Church services in the middle-
                west were held in New Sweden Settlement by a lay preacher,
                Magnus Fredrik Hokanson, who, in 1853, was formally or-
                dained a minister of the Swedish-American Lutheran
                Church.

January 24   Gold was discovered at Sutter's Fort in California, and
                shortly thereafter announcements of the California gold
                find began to appear in Denmark, Norway and Sweden.
                Gold fever spread throughout Scandinavia, and for a
                while California became synonomous with America. As
                time passed, the fever diminished, and Scandinavians re-
                sumed their regular migrations to the middle-west.

February   Johan Reierson founded a second colony in Texas in Van
                  Zandt and Kaufman counties, not far from Dallas. It was
                  called Prairieville.

April   The first Norwegian to go to the gold diggings in California
                  was Christian Poulsen, who had moved to San Francisco
                  from the mid-west as early as 1844. Poulsen's exagger-
                  ated accounts of the California gold fields thrilled Norwe-
                  gians who now wished to emigrate to America more than
                  ever.

April 21   Ulla Dalander was married to Johan Cassel, a son of Peter
                  Cassel, at Fairfield, Iowa. It was the first Swedish wedding
                  west of the Mississippi River.

June   A Koshkonong settler, Even O. Gullord, founded the well-
                  known Coon Prairie Settlement in Vernon County, Wiscon-
                  sin.

June   Many of the colonists at "Bishop Hill" found Eric Janson's
                  regime too autocratic in an economic sense. They also
                  began to tire of communal living as well as the rigid social
                  and religious rules, particularly his requirement, during
                  the first two years, that celibacy be observed by everyone,
                  including married couples. In June, the ban against matri-
                  mony was lifted and mass weddings took place.

August   Seven families of the second group that had emigrated from
                  Kisa, Sweden, finally reached the mid-west at Andover, Il-
                  linois, where they were invited to stay on by two Swedish
                  settlers, Hurtig and Samuel Samuelson. As an inducement
                  to settle in Andover, they had been offered free transporta-
                  tion to the town.

September 30   A number of Norwegians from Voss, living in Chicago,
                  formed a Correspondence Society, the chief object of which
                  was to send "America Letters" to Norway. This associa-
                  tion is also of interest because it was an early example of
                  a type of organization that was to become very common
                  among Norwegian-Americans........the Bygdelags or dis-
                  trict leagues which fostered social and cultural purposes
                  among emigrants and their descendents.

October   Jonas Hedström of Victoria, Illinois visited "Bishop Hill,"
                  remonstrated with Janson, and took back with him to Vic-
                  toria about 250 dissident members of the colony. They
                  settled at Victoria and Galesburg, many of them joining
                  Hedström's Swedish Methodist Church.

October 13   The bulk of the second group from Kisa, who had been induced to emigrate by Peter Cassel's letters, never reached New Sweden colony. Instead, they were diverted from the mid-west, and founded a permanent settlement at Sugar Grove in northern Pennsylvania, which by late 1848 was extended to Jamestown, New York. This colony became the largest and most homogeneously Swedish settlement in New York State.

1849

Norwegian emigration leaped from 1,400 in 1848 to 4,000 in 1849, the highest total up to that time.

Gustaf Unonius left Pine Lake Settlement and went to Chicago where he built the first Swedish church in that city, and became a clergyman of the American Protestant Episcopal faith. But, finding the Lutheran sentiment of his countrymen in Chicago too strong, he returned to Sweden in 1859 a bitterly disappointed man.

1849

The Danish-born Reverend C. L. Clausen wrote to Governor Ramsey of Minnesota asking him to allow Norwegians and Danes to settle in this vast new territory. Ramsey replied affirmatively, and a considerable settlement was destined to be established.

March   The cholera epidemic of this year ravaged the mid-west, and the Scandinavian settlements in Wisconsin and Illinois were attacked with full force.

March 6   Norwegian shipping interests were quick to take cognizance of the new possibilities for passenger traffic after the California gold find became widely known in Norway.

May 26   Marcus Thrane, the famous Norwegian labor organizer and reformer, urged everyone with small prospects in Norway to emigrate to America.

July   Cholera struck the "Bishop Hill" colony, brought there by three visiting Norwegian immigrants. One hundred and fourteen Swedes died, including Mrs. Janson and two of her children.

September 6   The pioneer Swedish Lutheran pastor in the mid-west was the Reverend Lars Paul Esbjörn, who arrived in New York with a large party of emigrants.   He and his following took up residence in Andover, Illinois.

October   S. M. Svensson of Texas became the first American emigration promotor in Sweden, bringing fifty young men back with him to Texas.

October   Reverend Esbjörn began organizing Swedish-Lutheran congregations at Andover, Galesburg, Princeton, and Moline, Illinois, and thus laid the foundations for what was to become the Augustana Synod.   He is regarded as the father of the Swedish-Lutheran Church in the United States.

1850

The census revealed that less than 600 Danes had entered the United States during the previous decade, and only some 1,800 had arrived in America between 1820-1850.

Danish immigration to America did not really begin until about mid-nineteenth century, when information concerning the economic opportunities available in the United States began to seep into the Danish peninsula from Norway and Germany.

1850

A more significant migration from Denmark began in 1850. It was inspired by Mormon missionaries who were active in Denmark from the early 1840's on.   Between 1850-1860, no less than 2,600 Danish Mormons migrated to the Mormon colonies in the west.   They were the forerunners of the 30,000 Danes who later came to the Mormon lands in Utah.

The actual figures of Scandinavians living in America were reported in the census of 1850: Norway, 12,678; Sweden, 3,559; Denmark, 1,837; total, 18,074.   Most of the Norse people lived at this time, in Wisconsin, and Illinois, but population returns of 28 states and 4 territories reported Norwegian inhabitants, and 12 states reported Swedish residents including 48 in Texas, 753 in New York, and 133 in Pennsylvania in addition to the midwest contingents.

Norwegians began to move into the northern tier of Iowa Counties, particularly Winneshiek, and into the southeastern counties of Minnesota in appreciable numbers.

By 1914, there were more Norwegians in Minnesota than in any other state.

Various Protestant groups made heavy inroads upon the Swedish Lutherans. By 1850, there were Swedish Methodist Churches in Illinois, organized into four circuits with six preachers. Jonas Hedström, the blacksmith-preacher, pioneered in this work of winning Swedes in Illinois for Methodism.

John Root, a Stockholm adventurer, who had married Eric Janson's cousin, shot Janson in an Illinois courthouse where a trial concerning his status in the "Bishop Hill" colony was in progress.

January 19   Early in 1850, the first steps were taken toward an organized expedition of gold seekers from Norway, and a sequence of events were set in motion that eventuated in a strange and unexpected experiment in colonization. Three men, O. Eide, A. Finne, and N. C. Tischendorff of Levanger, conceived the idea of an expedition to California financed and equipped through the sale of shares.

January 25   Hans Mattson arrived at Galesburg, Illinois, where he worked in the neighborhood with pick and shovel for $.75 to $1.00 a day on a railroad gang.

1850

April 25   A number of "Bishop Hill" Swedes arrived at Fort Kearney, California, having been afflicted with gold fever. Among them was Jonas Olsson, the brother of Olaf Olsson, one of the founders of "Bishop Hill." As far as known, the whole venture was a failure.

September   Fredrika Bremer, Sweden's most important novelist arrived in Minnesota as the guest of the governor of the state J. S. Ramsey. Miss Bremer's exceptional work, Homes of the New World came out of this trip through the Scandinavian areas of the United States. In glowing terms, she spoke to her fellow Scandinavians of the upper midwest. Probably no other book, before or after, has had such an important influence on prompting emigration from all the Scandinavian countries to the United States.

A Norwegian Moravian communistic experiment was initiated among a group of new immigrants in Wisconsin.

September 11 The famous showman and entrepreneur P. T. Barnum brought Jenny Lind, the great Swedish singer to the United States. Known as the "Swedish Nightingale," she made her American debut at Castle Garden in New York City.

October   The first log cabin built by Swedes in Minnesota was erected at Haylake in Washington County by three young Swedes who had moved there from Illinois. They were Carl Fernstrom, Oscar Roos, and August Sandahl.

October 19 The Levanger expedition financed by 200 shareholders bought a ship, the Sophie, and left for San Francisco with 106 passengers by way of Rio de Janeiro and Cape Horn. The ship broke down after it reached Rio in January, 1851. Some of the Norwegians joined a German colony in Brazil, while others left independently for California. A few of the goldseekers amassed moderate fortunes in California, but, in general, the Levanger expedition was a failure.

1851

Norwegians, Swedes, and Danes began pushing into Minnesota in large numbers after the Indian Treaties of 1851 had opened up these lands to settlement. In addition, immigration to these areas was facilitated by the advance of the railroads to the Mississippi at Rock Island, Illinois (1854), East Dubuque, Iowa, (1855), Prairie Du Chien, Wisconsin (1857), and La Crosse, Minnesota (1858).

1851

The Illinois-Central Railroad maintained "Swedish-Norwegian Land Agencies" and had their agents visit the Scandinavian villages, attend church in order to talk with the parishioners after the service about America, arrange farmers' meetings, attend county fairs, and in other ways seek to prove to prospective immigrants that the United States flowed with milk and honey.

Jonas Olson, en route to California to prospect for gold, turned homeward toward "Bishop Hill" to assume leadership of the now leaderless colony.

The first Norwegian church paper appeared, and continued to be published, with some interruptions and under various names, up to the outbreak of World War I.

Reverend Esbjörn succeeded in getting substantial gifts from Jenny Lind, for his plans to establish pioneer churches among the Swedes.

January   The colonists at "Bishop Hill," through cooperative efforts, were growing quite prosperous.   In addition to making all the goods they needed themselves, the Jansonites produced some items for sale.   For instance, 28,322 yards of linen cloth were woven from flax grown on the colony's land, and 3,237 yards of carpets were produced from the community's own materials.

January 15   Although the Swedes were relatively few in numbers, they organized the first Scandinavian political organization, the Swedish-American Republican Club of Illinois.

March   Nils Otto Tank, son of a distinguished Norwegian family, purchased 969 acres of land at Green Bay, Wisconsin. He moved a group of Norwegian Moravians from Milwaukee to this land, and established the colony of Ephraim.   The colony never succeeded.

June   A Moravian minister from Norway, A. M. Iverson, established an academy at the Tank colony at Green Bay.   It was the first high school established by Norwegians in America.

September   The Danish minister C. L. Clausen continued to establish settlements in the mid-west.   In the fall of 1851, he founded a colony of Norwegians in the northern part of Wisconsin in St. Croix and Pierce counties.

                Daniel Larsen and about 60 skilled Swedish workmen settled in Brockton, Massachusetts, to become the nucleus for the Swedish element in the shoe industry located there.

1852

Additional Mormon overseas missions were established in all the Scandinavian countries.   By 1861, several thousand Scandinavian Mormons had emigrated to the United States under close church supervision.   They all migrated to the Great Salt Lake Valley in Utah.

Total emigration from the Scandinavian countries rose to almost 5,000 persons during this year.   During the next fifteen years, however, emigration from Scandinavia leveled off until the post-Civil War period.

Reverend Esbjörn was instrumental in bringing Pastor T. N. Hasselquist to the United States in 1852.   Hasselquist was to become extremely important in the development of Swedish Lutheranism in America.

About 100 Swedes moved to Jamestown, New York where they went to work in the mills and factories.

January

Norwegian immigration had by this time worked its way into Minnesota especially in the southern counties of Houston, and Fillmore. By 1860, numerous settlements had been formed chiefly in the south and southeast, and the number of Norwegian-born in Minnesota stood at 8,425.

May

Hundreds of Norwegians left Wisconsin and Illinois bound for the gold fields of California. None ever really struck it rich, and many returned to their former homes. A few stayed on to farm in the rich Sacramento Valley region.

September

Swedish immigrants began arriving in ships carrying cargoes of iron to New York. The passage fee was $12 to $15 per person, provided the immigrant furnished his own food.

September 7

In Norway, as elsewhere, plans were made for transporting large numbers of emigrants to found a settlement in America where the culture and customs of the homeland would be recreated. The most noted example of such a plan among the Norwegians was the project of the famous Norwegian violinist, Ole Bull, to establish in Pennsylvania a colony called Oleana. Chicanery by local land speculators, and mismanagement by Bull, himself, doomed the ill-fated project in 1853. But the failure of Oleana did not dampen Norway's appetite for emigration. It merely confirmed her people in their judgment that the Mississippi Valley was their more natural habitat.

1853

The ballad "Oleana" was written by a Norwegian newspaper editor, Ditmar Meidell, as a satirical thrust at the exaggerated claims made for Ole Bull's American colony.

1853

As Norwegian emigration to the United States grew during the 1850's, foreign shipping companies established agencies and sent "emigrant runners" to a number of cities in Norway. The same situation prevailed in Denmark and Sweden during these years.

A Norwegian newspaper was established in Chicago to serve the needs of the growing Norwegian population in and around the city.

Hasselquist's first congregation in the United States was located at Galesburg, Illinois. He was a typical pioneer preacher who worked hard among the scattered Swedish settlements to counteract the inroads of the proselyting sects.

February   An important Norwegian colony was established in central Iowa focusing in Story County. This was an example of deliberate colonization. In fact, throughout the late 1850's Scandinavians began streaming into Iowa from both the Old Country and from other settlements in the mid-west.

March   "Bishop Hill" colony was incorporated by the laws of Illinois, the charter giving almost unlimited power to a board of seven trustees.

Ole Canuteson, a farmer from the Fox River colony in Illinois founded another Norwegian settlement in Texas in Bosque County, a short distance from Waco. This was to become the most important Norwegian colony in Texas, but as of 1853, there were only 105 Norwegians in the entire state.

April   A caravan of some forty canvas-covered wagons drawn by oxen brought 40 Norwegian families to a new colony in Iowa founded by Reverend Clausen. It was named St. Anagar.

1854

Net Swedish emigration reached a figure of a little over 2 per thousand of resident population, a figure not matched again until after the Civil War.

The Swedish population at New Sweden, Iowa had grown to 500, many of whom owned sizeable farms.

The shippers of Göteborg, Sweden, were overwhelmed with people clamoring for passage to the United States. Since direct sailing vessels could not convey the throng of Swedish emigrants, the overflow made their way to America via Hamburg or Hull to Liverpool.

A missionary society, supported by the Methodist Episcopal Church was organized for the expressed purpose of working among Swedish immigrants.

June   Not all Scandinavian immigrants went west. A number of them remained in New York City where they had arrived from Europe. In New York, they tended to settle on the eastside of Manhattan, particularly in the Fourth and Seventh Wards, and in the business districts at the lower tip of the island.

November   Scandinavians, as a group, began to transfer their political allegiance from the Democratic to the Republican Party. The festering argument over slavery was convincing Scandinavians that their basic beliefs were more closely akin to Republican Party philosophy. Yet, except among the Swedes, the process of transformation was by no means complete until 1860.

Fifty three newly arrived Norwegian Mormons arrived at the Mormon settlement at Great Salt Lake in Utah.

1855

The New York State Census showed 8.62 percent of all Scandinavians living in New York City were gainfully employed in the building trades, 12.03 percent in the clothing industry, 5 percent were laborers, 10 percent were engaged in maritime pursuits, and 2.67 percent were transportation workers.

Hasselquist established the Hemlandet and the Rätta Hemlandet, a religious paper, primarily to combat the proselyters in the west, and to preserve the true Lutheran faith. He founded Sunday schools and parochial schools, sometimes meeting with his flock in barns in the early years.

A few Swedish families moved into Kansas, although the greater Swedish migration to this state would take place after the Civil War.

Wisconsin, Iowa and Michigan had small Swedish settlements, and about 500 Swedes had settled near Lafayette, Indiana.

February   The first Norwegian church in Texas was erected at Prairieville under the ministership of A. E. Frederichsen who had arrived in the United States in 1854.

September 11   Seventy-one Swedish and four hundred and nine Danish Mormons arrived in the United States. Their destination was Great Salt Lake Basin in Utah.

1856

Most Norwegian newspapers became Republican papers, but editors like Gabriel Bjornson and Jacob Seeman, and newspapers like <u>Den Norske Amerikaner</u> and <u>Nordstjernen</u> remained Democratic in the 1850's.

January   Step by step the Jansonite colony at "Bishop Hill" acquired more and more land until by this date, the community owned 8,500 acres in Illinois.

February   Iowa population statistics revealed that by the late winter of 1856, more than 800 Norwegians and more than 100 Swedes had made this state their new home.

April   A group of religious dissenters known as Haugeans, who had originally come from Norway and settled at the Fox River colony in Illinois, moved to Story County, Iowa and set up a new settlement which they named "Palestine." They were led by Osmund Sheldal, Ole Flatland, Ole Apland, and Osmund Johnson. The sect had been founded in Norway by Hans Nielsen Hauge, who believed in saving souls, and who disliked the Norwegian state church.

May 1   Two hundred and forty emigrants from Poraguind, Norway were drawn to California by the continuing lure of gold.

June   Knud Pederson, a Mormon missionary from Utah, brought 600 Scandinavians back with him to Great Salt Lake Valley after a successful conversion trip through Norway, Sweden, and Denmark.

November 4   The bulk of the Scandinavian-Americans cast their votes for the Republican Party's candidates including John C. Fremont who had been nominated for the presidency. Many of them refused to support the Democratic Party's platform which upheld the Kansas-Nebraska Act as the only sound and safe solution of the slavery question. Moreover, like most immigrants, they were opposed to the American (Know-Nothing) Party's candidate because of his support for immigration restriction, and longer residence requirements for citizenship.

December   Desertions of Scandinavian seamen continued and reached alarming proportions. Between 1856 and 1865, 11,000 Swedes and Norwegians left their ships, and after the Civil War the numbers were still higher.

1857

By this date, there were half a dozen rapidly growing Danish communities in Wisconsin. The most important of these was Racine, founded in 1834, and which in time came to be known as Dane City. It was the center of Danish cultural influence throughout the midwest.

Swedish-Americans established many other societies for benevolent and cultural purposes as soon as the first stages of pioneering were past and time was available for things other than work. In 1857, several of these organizations were formed in cities of the mid-west.

Peter Laurentius Larsen first came to the United States in 1857 and preached among the pioneers of Wisconsin. He is often called the "Nestor" of the Norwegian Lutherans.

March — John Erik Lindmark, a Swede who arrived in the United States in 1800, and became a very prosperous merchant in New York City, devised a sincere if fantastic plan for a League of Nations.

April — The patriotic Svea Society was formed in Chicago by diverse Scandinavian immigrants. It wholeheartedly supported the Republican Party, and was the first of its kind among Scandinavian-Americans.

July — A dispute arose in Madison, Wisconsin concerned with the Norwegian immigrants' observation of the "Continental Sunday" as compared with the native-Americans' more solemn observation of the so-called "American Sunday." In this dispute, Norwegian clergymen took the side of the natives, and forbade the faithful to observe the Sabbath as they had in the Old Country, so as to conform to the "American System," and not bring the Norwegian Church into disrepute.

August 24 — The Panic of 1857 struck the United States causing severe hardship among Scandinavian immigrants in the middle-west. The Panic and subsequent depression discouraged Scandinavian emigration, and a sharp downward trend in emigration from the whole of Scandinavia resulted.

December 4 — The Swedish settlers at "Bishop Hill" were especially hard hit by the Panic of 1857, and in order to offset the financial crisis, they had to borrow money, for the first time, against their collective land-holdings.

1858

Swedish and Norwegian emigration to the United States stirred self-criticism in the Old World, and helped in the movement for social legislation, labor reform, and political liberation.

In 1858, a small colony of Danish immigrants was established at Racine, Wisconsin. Most of the Danish settlers went to the states of the agricultural west.

The Swedish Lutheran Church in America had 13 ministers and 28 congregations and was strongest in Illinois and Minnesota. The total membership at that time probably did not exceed 3,000.

March   Laurentius Larsen, the Norwegian pastor of the Rush River Settlement in Wisconsin, made an extended missionary journey into Minnesota, visiting the new settlements, and organizing about a half dozen Norwegian Lutheran congregations.

1859

A number of Norwegians found employment in the lead mines located in the village of Wiota, Lafayette County, Wisconsin. They stayed in the mines only long enough to get cash for the down payment on a piece of farm land.

The Swedish Publication Society, founded by Pastor T. N. Hasselquist, was transferred to Chicago from Galesburg, Illinois. It supplied the Lutheran churches with religious works, parochial school texts, and hymnals, such as the Swedish Psalmbook, and the Hemlandssänger, which ran through a number of editions.

Andreas Tjernagel came to America and settled in Iowa at a town called Story City. He, his children and grandchildren formed the famous and unique Fallinglo Orchestra, named after their home in Valders, Norway.

January   "Bishop Hill" Swedes had fully recovered from the Panic of 1857, paid off their loans, and had their assets appraised at $770,000, most of which was in the form of land.

THE ERA OF MASS IMMIGRATION
(1860-1910)

1860

The census of 1860 revealed that 72,000 people of Scandinavian birth were residents of the United States by the eve of the Civil War: 44,000 Norwegians, 18,000 Swedes, and 10,000 Danes. More than half of these people were located in Wisconsin, and virtually all the rest were in Illinois, Iowa and Minnesota. The census also indicated that the number of Swedish immigrants was increasing more rapidly than the other two Scandinavian groups, and was soon destined to outrun Norwegian immigration to America.

By 1860, there were more than 10,000 Norwegians in Illinois, mainly in the region around Chicago.

By 1860, about 2,000 Danes had been attracted to the Great Salt Lake Basin by Mormon missionaries.

By 1860, no less than six Norwegian synodical organizations were established in the United States. However, unity was hard to maintain, and many Norwegian Lutherans became closely affiliated with the Missouri Synod of the German Lutheran group.

By 1860, there were 30,000 Norwegians scattered throughout the southern half of the state of Wisconsin, the majority of them concentrated in Dane, Vernon (then known as Bad Ax), Columbia, and La Crosse Counties.

The California census showed that despite the lure of gold, only 715 Norwegians, 327 Swedes, and 124 Danes were in that state. The permanent interest among the Scandinavians was in fertile farming land.

By 1860, the only two states in the Union that did not have Norwegian immigrants were Vermont and Delaware.

In 1860, the Scandinavian Evangelical Lutheran Augustana Synod was organized with Reverend Hasselquist as president. A plea was made for money from the fatherland and a seminary to train ministers was opened in a Norwegian Lutheran church in Chicago.

By 1860, the Swedish settlements on the prairies of Illinois extended like a belt, west and southwest, from Lake Michigan to the Mississippi River, with special Swedish centers at Rockford, Rock Island, Moline, Swedona, Geneva, Galesburg, and in Henry and Kane Counties.

1860

By 1860, Chicago was the geographical center of Swedish-America, and Swedish was spoken on the streets until well past 1870.

By 1860, the number of Swedish Lutheran congregations had risen to 39, the number of preachers to 17, and the number of communicants to nearly 5,000.

Campaign orators were employed by the Republican National Committee to spread the faith in the Swedish tongue, and Swedish-American newspapers were held in their staunch alliance to the Republican party by a systematic apportionment of paid political advertisements at election time.

January   By the beginning of the decade of the sixties, Scandinavians were rapidly moving into Minnesota from their older settlements in Iowa, Illinois and Wisconsin. Due to the extension of the railroads, and official and unofficial propaganda for settlers, Scandinavians in Minnesota increased from 12 in 1850 to 12,000 by 1860.

February   The first Swedish church was organized in San Francisco.

A foreshadowing of an important trend was the presence of 129 Norwegians in the Dakota Territory, living in and about the town of Vermillion, and up the Missouri River. By 1940, so many Norwegians were residing in North and South Dakota that this element constituted a larger percentage of their respective state populations than even in the population of Minnesota.

March   The Swedish-Norwegian government abolished passport regulation and the last serious obstacle to emigrant departure was removed.

July   Norwegians, as a group, refused to endorse the pro-slavery position that had been taken by leading Norwegian Lutheran clergymen who had fallen under the influence of the German Lutheran Missouri Synod.

October   Swedish-Americans took a fierce anti-slavery stand in the critical sectional struggle going on in the United States. The leader of the Swedish immigrants in this feeling was the Reverend T. N. Hasselquist.

1860

November 6   Even before the presidential election of 1860, Norwegians
               and Swedes had shown partiality toward Abraham Lincoln.
               In the slavery debates, particularly those of Lincoln and
               Stephen A. Douglas, these Scandinavians manifested a
               keen interest. Their two influential newspapers Hemland-
               et (Swedish) published at Galesburg and Chicago, Illinois,
               and Emigranten (Norwegian) published at Madison, Wiscon-
               sin, consistently defended Lincoln and the Republican Party.
               And, on election day, the Republicans and Lincoln owed
               much to the well-nigh solid Swedish vote in Illinois and
               the Norwegian vote in Wisconsin and Minnesota. Among
               the Scandinavians, Lincoln had many friends and some party
               workers. In Rockford, Illinois, for example, 80 of them
               marched to the polls in a body, led by their ministers, to
               vote for Lincoln. The Scandinavian who refused to vote
               for Lincoln in 1860 was indeed a rare specimen.

December   The Norwegians in America have at various times founded,
               maintained and lost almost every kind of school. In
               1860, they founded their first Academy in the United
               States, and during the next thirty years academies and sec-
               ondary religious schools were established in more than
               fifty different communities. Few of them survived for
               more than ten years, and by 1900 there were practically
               none left in the country.

1861

               By this time, the Norwegian Lutheran Synod in America
               had 69 formally accepted congregations and its ministers
               actually served an additional 21.

               Norwegians in Wisconsin were selling their wheat for 62¢
               a bushel and oats for 25¢. Anders and Ole Jensen Stor-
               toen of Pierce County wrote that they were making the
               fabulous sum of $1 a day.

September 1   The Norwegians founded their first college in America;
               Luther College located in Decorah, Iowa. Its first Presi-
               dent was Laur Larsen, who remained in that position until
               1902, during which time his influence upon the course of
               education, and no less upon religious development, among
               Norwegian immigrants and their children was exceedingly
               important.

September 16   The American Civil War was the first national event in
               which the Swedish immigrants took part. One of the first

Swedish immigrant communities to organize a military unit to fight for the Union was "Bishop Hill." This unit was incorporated into the Illinois state troops in the fall of 1861. One of the officers was Eric Johnson, the son of the founder, Eric Jansen, and the unit was called the 56th Regiment of Illinois Infantry Volunteers.

1861

Colonel Oscar Malmborg, who had served eight years in the Swedish Army and also in the Mexican War, commanded the 55th, Illinois Volunteers. Other Swedish-American officers of note who served in the Civil War were Captains Axel Silfverspaire, Frederick Spairestrom, C. E. Landstrom, Andrew Stenbeck, and Andrew G. Warner; and Colonels O. P. Vegesack, R. V. Steelhammar, J. S. Eliving, and Oscar Brydolf.

Abraham Lincoln appointed the Swedish-American, Charles J. Sundell of Chicago as American consul to Stettin, Germany.

Thirteen hundred Swedish volunteers entered the Union Army from Illinois, which had a total Swedish population of 7,000 in 1861.

November   While the "Bishop Hill" company was the most homogeneously Swedish in the Union armies, other Swedish communities in Iowa, Wisconsin and Minnesota, as well as Illinois, furnished predominantly Swedish units for service in the Civil War.

December   Norwegian-Americans participated actively in the Civil War, volunteering for local army units by the hundreds. They usually served in the ranks, and only a small few became officers. Unlike the Swedes they did not form their own ethnic companies. The highest ranking Norwegian in the Union army was Colonel Hans Christian Heg of the Muskego Settlement.

1862

As a result of the establishment of Luther College, and the influence of the Decorah Posten, the town of Decorah, Iowa became the most important cultural center for Norwegians in the United States.

Company D of the 3rd Minnesota regiment was an exclusively Scandinavian outfit, commanded by Hans Mattson.

The 15th Wisconsin Infantry contained many Swedish, Norwegian and Danish volunteers. They participated in a number of the battles in the west under the general command of U. S. Grant.

March 9   In the United States Navy during the Civil War, many officers and sailors of Scandinavian birth or descent performed valuable services, but the two most prominent were Admiral J. A. Dahlgren, inventor of the guns that bear his name, and Captain John Ericsson, whose ship, the ironclad, Monitor, the first to use a revolving turret, stopped the Confederate ironclad, Merrimac in a five hour battle off the Virginia coast. Ericsson was also an inventor of some note, his most famous creation being a new screw propeller for ships.

April 6   The Swedish volunteers from "Bishop Hill" fought in the battles of Fort Donelson, and Shiloh, distinguishing themselves valiantly. Major Eric Forsse was their company commander.

May 20   The Homestead Act was passed by Congress giving 160 acres of land free to any settler. The Federal and State governments, railroads, steamship lines, and land companies worked feverishly at home and abroad to bring people to America. Norway and Sweden's dispirited farmers answered the call, streaming to the offices of government officials and shipping lines to secure emigration permits and tickets.

Homestead legislation and the liberal attitude of the western states toward immigrants were important factors in starting the Danish immigrant tide to the United States. Religious controversies in Denmark also played their part but, as in the case of other Scandinavians, the economic urge was dominant.

November 12 In addition to the Swedes who were already fighting in the Union army, thousands of men still in Sweden offered to enlist in the Union cause. The American consul in Stockholm reported that there were more than 2,000 applications.

1863

Marcus Thrane emigrated to America and opened a new chapter in his career in the west. In time, he became very active in the interests of the poor and downtrodden as an editor and writer. Thrane also aided the development of the American labor movement.

There was a company of Swedes under Captain H. Arosenius in the 43rd Illinois regiment, and another under Captain O. R. Corneliuson in the 23rd Wisconsin regiment.

Reverend Hasselquist signed a contract with the Illinois Central Railroad to sell land on commission to settlers, in order to get Swedes out of the cities and bring them into the farming communities of Illinois. The seminary cleared $14,000 in five years from his activity as land agent for the railroad.

March   The first Danes arrived in Iowa, and within a short time there were several flourishing Danish colonies in that state, centering in Shelby, Case, and Audubon Counties. Before the close of the century, there were 13,000 Danish speaking people in these counties. So predominantly Danish were these communities, that, in time, the handful of Scotch and Irish settlers living there, came to speak Danish as a second language.

1863

May   Anton M. Holter, a Norwegian, usually credited with being the first Scandinavian in Montana, made a fortune in lumbering in and around Helena. He also added to his wealth by accumulating numerous mining interests throughout the state.

September 19 Colonel Hans Christian Heg was killed at the battle of Chickamauga, and became the symbol of the Norwegian-American's contribution to the Civil War.

September 30 Throughout the Civil War, American agents in Scandinavian countries were instructed to spread information about opportunities to acquire land, and otherwise earn a living in the United States. The Homestead Act was used as the best argument.

November   The Norwegian government finally passed an act to regulate emigration to the United States.

1864

Charles John Stolbrand, who organized a Swedish battery in De Kalb, Illinois, rose to the rank of Brigadier General.

Niels Paulson, a Dane who came to the United States in 1864, became a wealthy builder and ironmaster. With part of his earnings, he endowed the American-Scandina-

vian Foundation to foster closer relations between the
United States and the Scandinavian countries.

The economic crisis of 1864 in Sweden was followed by
three years of crop failures, and "The Great Famine" remained a vivid memory in Sweden for many years leading
to an exodus of thousands of bankrupt landowners and agricultural laborers to the United States.

Norwegian and Swedish Lutherans established their own
churches and synods. It was an indication, that, in deter-
mining religious groupings, doctrinal matters were sometimes less important than differences of language and geographical origin. They also established parochial schools
believing that instruction in the mother tongue was essential
to the preservation of religious belief. Neither the Norwegians or the Swedes were ever wholly successful in their
aims, because of lack of funds and trained teachers, and the
majority sent their children to the public schools.

June   By 1864, Eric Janson was dead, and the membership of
              the "Bishop Hill" colony shrunk to 655 people of whom 172
              were minors.

                              1864

June   A Methodist Congregation was organized at "Bishop Hill"
              as Jansonism was rapidly fading from the scene.

July   The first Danish Baptist publishing house was established,
              and shortly afterwards a hymn book written in the Danish
              language was published in Iowa.

August   Andrew G. Warner, a native of northern Halsingland, Swe-
              den, volunteered to command a company in the Sixty-Third
              Colored Infantry, a unit formed out of ex-slaves. It
              was quite a dangerous post, as the Confederates swore to
              shoot on sight any white man commanding Negro troops.

December 21   The Swedish regiment took part in General William T.
              Sherman's famous "March to the Sea." They reached
              Savannah on this day and then proceeded northward into
              the Carolinas.

                              1865

              By the end of the Civil War, it was estimated that between
              3,000 and 4,000 Swedes fought in the Union Army.

Cleng Peerson, who had shown great enthusiasm for Norwegian emigration to Texas died in Bosque County, Texas.   He had exercised a greater influence upon early Norwegian immigration and settlement than any other man.

By 1865, the Augustana Synod had dispatched missionaries
to Montreal, Quebec and New York to meet incoming immigrants and direct them to Illinois.

Although Scandinavians did not venture into the South in
great numbers, a few Scandinavian settlements were established in that region, such as the Swedish town of Stockholm near Richmond, Virginia.

Many of the first Swedish settlers in Nebraska were attracted by the Union Pacific Railroad shops built in Omaha,
which provided employment for blacksmiths, machinists,
and carpenters.

The "American Fever" lured 10,000 immigrants from
Norway, Sweden and Denmark during this year.   They
left directly from their own countries, traveled by land
or water to Hamburg, Germany, or crossed the North Sea
to Hull, whence they continued by rail through England to
Liverpool.

January 24   The Swedish Regiment fought in the final battle of the
              Georgia campaign, helping to defeat the Confederates near
              the Savannah River.

March   S. M. Svensson organized a special agency to promote emi-
              gration from Sweden to Texas.   A system of contract labor,
              bordering on indentured servitude was employed, and hun-
              dreds of Swedes entered the United States in this manner.

July 1   The first native born Swede to be appointed a cadet at
              West Point was Eric Bergland, a son of Andrew Bergland,
              one of the original trustees of "Bishop Hill."

September   A Danish Baptist Congregation was organized in Potter
              County, Pennsylvania, and the following years witnessed
              the establishment of a dozen other Danish Baptist com-
              munities scattered throughout the middle-west.   Many
              Danes began to emigrate to America from 1865 on, be-
              cause during the following years, the Danish government
              was notably illiberal with respect to religion.

November   Marcus Thrane moved to Chicago and started a newspaper
              Den Norsk Amerikaner, through which he continued to voice
              his social and political beliefs.

1866

After the Civil War came to a close, a Lincoln-worship was assiduously cultivated by the Republican party among the Swedish Voters.

Two leading Norwegian secular newspapers were founded; Decorah Posten (Decorah, Iowa), and Skandinaven (Chicago, Illinois). They both spanned the period of heaviest Norwegian immigration, and were politically independent. Iver Larsen Boe, the founder of Skandinaven, made that paper into a real power in the mid-west.

Fifteen thousand Norwegians came to the United States, an increase of 11,000 over the previous year. This gave warning that a period of mass emigration had begun.

Between 1866 and 1873, 11,896 Norwegians settled in the United States.

1867

More than 1600 Danes left the province of Schleswig after that area had been conquered by Prussia in the Danish-German War of the previous year. Most of them came to the mid-west and Pennsylvania.

1867

The Norwegian government passed a law which tried to restrict the emigration of men owing military service, men deserting their families, and debtors. There were many other restrictions, but the statute did not appreciably decrease emigration. At about the same time, Sweden enacted similar regulations. They, too, failed.

1868

A few Philadelphians of Scandinavian birth founded the Scandinavian Society of Philadelphia, regarded by the members as a continuation of the original society founded in 1759.

The Swedes began coming in appreciable numbers reaching the 5,000 mark in 1868.

Brynhild Amundsen reached Decorah, Iowa, with his press, and all his other possessions in two wagons. He soon began to publish a newspaper that was to become an important Scandinavian American organ.

The first Norwegian newspaper in Minnesota was opened at Rochester in 1868. It was called the Nordiske Folksblad.

April

In Chicago, a group of recently arrived Swedish immigrants, under the leadership of Sven August Lindell, formed a stock company called "The First Swedish Agricultural Company," the purpose of which was to acquire a large tract of land somewhere in the west for an exclusively Swedish and Lutheran community. The area they eventually chose was located in the Smokey River Valley in Kansas.

1869

Missouri was opened to Swedish settlement by the Missouri Land Company, which was a subsidiary of the Swedish Commercial Company which had helped to settle Kansas.

Eric Forsse, of Civil War fame, and fifty other Swedish farmers left Illinois, and moved further west to Kansas, where they took up land in a community they called Falun.

The Freja Society, a male chorus of 60 voices was organized in Chicago as a singing society for Swedes and Norwegians.

The earliest and most prominent Swedish-born official American promoter of emigration from Sweden to the United States, especially Minnesota, was Hans Mattson.

He was appointed secretary and general manager of the Minnesota Immigration Board. Every state in the midwest established Immigration Boards to promote Scandinavian as well as other immigration to their lands.

April

Railroad companies also began to advertise for immigrants so as to sell the millions of acres of land they had been granted by the Federal government during the construction of their lines. Mattson acted as an agent for the Northern Pacific Railroad, and brought a group of 800 Scandinavians to settle in Minnesota.

Knute Steenerson went west into the Minnesota River Valley beyond the pale of white settlement. He staked out his claim in Lac qui Paile County. After a few years, a flourishing Norwegian settlement extended fifty miles along the Minnesota River Valley, with Montevideo as its center.

July   The Minnesota Board of Immigration employed Paul Hjelm
                Hansen, a Norwegian journalist, to explore the Red River
                region in an effort to attract immigrants.

December   In order to promote immigration to America, several
                special Swedish newspapers were published beginning in
                1869 and extending into the early 1870's. Among them
                were Amerike, Nya Werlden, and Amerika-Bladet.

1870

The census revealed a Danish population of 30,000 in the
United States.

By 1870, there were less than 3,000 Danes in Iowa, many of
whom came from the German province of Schleswig-Holstein. All the important Danish settlements in Iowa were
started after the Civil War. The bulk of the immigrants
were farmers, agricultural laborers, and artisans who had
few resources other than a determination to succeed. Many
worked at first for the railroads, or for American farmers,
and some bought out Yankee farmers as soon as they had
saved enough to make the first payment. From the first,
the Danes emphasized dairying and were interested in cooperative creameries.

Scandinavians began to take up land under the Homestead
Act in earnest. Their major area of penetration was a
great triangle of land that included a region between the upper Mississippi and Missouri Rivers, with an extension
westward of the latter in its lower reaches.

C. Amundson, the former coachman of Governor Ramsey of
Minnesota was elected to the Minnesota state legislature.

1870

Since 1870, Minnesota had more Norwegians than any other
state in the union, although the Swedes outnumbered them in
the state as a whole.

The census of 1870 revealed that 90 percent of all the Norwegians in the United States were in Wisconsin, Minnesota,
Iowa and Northern Illinois.

In 1870, as a result of many controversies over doctrinal
matters, the Norwegians separated from the Augustana
Synod, and formed a Norwegian-Danish organization which,
a few years later, split into two independent synods.

In 1870, when the famous Swedish singer Christina Nilsson visited Chicago, there was almost a battle royal among the Swedish element in the city to determine which Swedish organization should sponsor the reception given in her honor.

From 1870 onward, Nebraska received Swedish stock as a result of the advertisements of railroad companies and the work of the Nebraska Immigration Board.

Andreas Veland, son of the Storting's most prominent bønde, Ole Garbill Veland emigrated to America in the fall of 1870. He was soon joined by thousands of other bønde in this post-Civil-War movement to the United States.

The Yellowstone division of the Northern Pacific was built largely by Scandinavian laborers who then settled along the route. Wages were seldom more than $1.50 a day, and sometimes less.

January   Norwegians did well in farming in Wisconsin. By 1870, more than 200 of them had farms of over 310 acres.

February   The last official action to bring in Swedish immigrants en masse, was made by the state of Maine under the direction of William Widgery Thomas who was then the State Commissioner of Immigration.

June   By this time, the Jansonite community at "Bishop Hill" numbered less than 500 residents. As a result, the community was dissolved, and a final division of property took place.

November   Worchester, Massachusetts received a sizeable influx of Swedish workers who found ready employment in this building industrial center.

1870

Claus Clausen represented the Scandinavians on the Iowa Board of Immigration which was established in 1870 to promote European emigration to that state.

A Danish dairying colony was organized in Mississippi, but went into oblivion after a few years.

November 3   Hans Mattson was elected Secretary of State of Minnesota. He was the first Scandinavian-American to reach such a high public office in the United States.

From 1870 on, Scandinavians began to enter state politics in Wisconsin, Minnesota, and the Dakotas, and by 1890, they commanded the major offices in Minnesota, as the native leaders of the Republican Party reluctantly yielded power.

1871

Between 1871 and 1875, Norwegian immigration was predominantly rural, and came mainly from the class of small peasant proprietors; the crafters, who were married agricultural workers, seldom were able to find money for passage, and the better situated farmers did not wish to leave the Old Country. After 1875, however, Norwegian emigration became more an urban and industrial rather than a rural phenomenon.

February   An attempt was made to unite the Norwegian Lutheran Church in America with the Swedish and Danish Lutheran Churches. This effort proved unsuccessful.

June   Rasmus Hannibal of Milwaukee formed the "Danish Land and Homestead Company," and in late summer a committee set out to explore the possibilities of organized colonization in Nebraska. Up to this time, the Danish migrations to America were, for the most part, highly individualistic affairs.

1872

Stromberg, Nebraska was founded by Illinois Swedes, and to the northwest a rural community known as Swedehome was established.

Like other Scandinavian-Americans, the Danes established their own foreign language press. The first Danish newspaper in the United States was Den Danske Pioneer. It was a liberal newspaper with socialistic tendencies, and in politics it supported the Democratic Party. Among some of the other papers of the Danish-American press were Bien (The Bee), published in 1880; Nordlyset, published in New York in 1880; Dansk Tidende (Danish Times), published in Chicago in 1892; Ugeblad, published in Tyler, Minnesota; and Luthersk Ugeblad, the official organ of the United Danish Lutheran Church, published in 1919.

July   The First Danish Lutheran Church was organized in the United States. It dominated the religious affiliations of the majority of Danish immigrants, and it is known today as the United Danish Evangelical Church.

August   The Republican organization distributed campaign litera-
              ture in Swedish throughout the state of Minnesota indicat-
              ing the growing importance of the Swedish vote in not only
              that state, but throughout the entire middle-west.

November 5   Eric Forsse became the first Scandinavian-American
              elected to the Kansas State Legislature.

              Reverend Hasselquist and the Hemlandet supported Grant,
              largely because the Liberal Republicans were supported by
              German liberals who favored "all kinds of liberty" includ-
              ing "Sabbath Liberty." The Swedish Lutherans exhibited
              definite conservative tendencies during this campaign.

              A large number of Scandinavians in the mid-west joined
              the liberal Republican movement in reaction away from the
              corruption of the Grant administration, and the Radical
              Republican policy toward the South. In the presidential
              election of 1872, many of them cast their ballots for the
              Liberal Republican candidate, Horace Greeley who was
              defeated by Ulysses S. Grant.

                                 1873

              One of the biggest attractions for Scandinavians in the
              Red River Valley of the Dakota Territory, especially
              single men, were the bonanza farms that flourished from
              1873 through the next twenty years.

                                 1874

              By 1874, there were ten Swedish newspapers being pub-
              lished in California, although most of them were short-
              lived.

              St. Olaf's College was founded by the Norwegians in North-
              field, Minnesota. It received its charter in 1889, and be-
              came the largest and best equipped of all the Norwegian-
              American colleges. Other institutions of higher learning
              were founded during the following years; Concordia College
              (Minnesota), Augustana College (South Dakota), and Pacific
              Lutheran College (Washington). In the establishment of all
              of these colleges the primary motive was to train candidates
              for the theological seminaries of the various church bodies.

              Jon Toreson, a Norwegian, better known as "Snow-shoe
              Thompson" retired. Toreson had left Illinois to rush to the
              California gold fields in 1850. Having failed to strike it
              rich, he got a job carrying the mail over the high Sierra

Mountains during the winter months. He made himself a pair of sturdy oak skis, and for the next 24 years was the only mail carrier between California and Nevada. Today his skis are in a museum in Sacramento, a tribute to this forerunner of the stage coach and the railroad.

May

The "Danish Land and Homestead Company", led by Rasmus Hannibal, found a desirable location in the central part of Nebraska at Grand Island. Danes began to flock into this region in considerable numbers. The towns of Danneborg and Nysted were established, a Folk High School was built, cooperative creameries were inaugurated, and a "little Denmark" came into existence.

1875

The Augustana College and Theological Seminary was transferred to Rock Island, Illinois, and has remained the center of Swedish Lutheran activities in the United States.

By 1875, Wisconsin was able to support a Danish paper, the Stjernen, which circulated in several Danish agricultural villages.

In certain townships in Western Wisconsin, Norwegians were so predominant that members of that group were employed as census takers, and they soon came to dominate most of the township offices. Between 1875 and 1885, they held more than half of the seats on the county board.

January

At the start of 1875, wheat had firmly established itself as the principal crop raised by the Norwegians in Wisconsin and Minnesota. However, at about this time, they began to adopt a new line of agriculture, dairy farming. Within a few years, they were leading the nation in the production of dairy prodcuts.

April

Olaf Hedstrom retired, and the Bethel Ship was now used for a few years as a mission for Danish and Norwegian immigrants rather than Swedish.

1876

Tobacco raising began to become a profitable business for Norwegian farmers in Wisconsin. They became the principal producers in the mid-west led by the major tobacco entrepreneur in the region, Andrew Jenson.

1876

From 1876 to 1881, Hans Mattson was editor-in-chief of the Minnesota Stats Tidning in Minneapolis, a newspaper highly favorable toward the Republican party.

January
Victor Lawson, a Norwegian, purchased the Chicago Daily News and became a power in American journalism. He led the Associated Press out of a serious crisis, and thereafter exercised a great influence upon the handling of foreign news.

Hans Mattson stumped the Scandinavian settlements of Minnesota in behalf of the Republican party and its candidate Rutherford B. Hayes of Ohio.

May
As power in the Republican Party shifted to eastern financial and industrial leadership, and the economic interests of the upper Mississippi region began their long descent from Republican policies, the Scandinavians began their insurgency within the Republican ranks. There were marked defections to the Greenback movement in Illinois, Wisconsin and Minnesota.

November 7
Despite their disaffection with the Republican Party, most Scandinavians apparently supported Rutherford B. Hayes for the presidency.

1877

The Norwegian-American Historical Museum was founded in Decorah, Iowa, which was now being called the "Norwegian Capital" of the state.

Carl Sandburg's father was August Johnson, a Swedish immigrant who settled in Illinois and changed his name because Illinois had so many other Johnsons in that period of heavy Scandinavian immigration.

As a rule, Swedish farmers were not enthusiastic over the Granger movement of the late 1860's and 1870's. Swedish and Norwegian Lutherans alike looked upon the Grangers as another secret society, Masonic in origin and anti-Christian. The opposition of the Lutheran Church was so strong that it may have been a real factor in the decline of the Granger strength in states like Iowa and Illinois.

March
The Danish socialist leaders, Louis Pio, and A. Geleff, found their way to Kansas, where they attempted to estab-

lish a socialist community at Hays City, a venture that met with disaster. The small group of Danish socialists who had attempted to settle there, then dispersed to different parts of the midwest.

1877

September 23 The Swedish Methodist churches in the northwest, which had hitherto been attached to several annual conferences, were combined as the Northwestern Swedish Annual Conference. Churches in Illinois, Michigan, Minnesota, Iowa, Kansas and Nebraska became affiliated with the new conference, although their membership at that time did not exceed 4,000.

1878

The Chicago, Milwaukee, and St. Paul Railroad extended the lines deep into the Minnesota River Valley, bringing with it hundreds of new Norwegian immigrants.

1879

The first Norwegian newspaper to be established in South Dakota was the Folkstidende published at Sioux Falls.

The second great post-Civil War Norwegian emigration began in 1879. Between 1879 and 1893, considered the peak years, 256,068 persons arrived in the United States. During this same period Swedish emigration amounted to well over 400,000.

June   Probably the earliest, and most prominent Norwegian immigrant to come to Oregon was Simon Benson. In 1915, he was honored as Oregon's first citizen.

1880

Beginning in 1880, Swedish mass emigration began. In fact, the peak decade for this group was the 1880's when so many Swedes emigrated to America that this movement nullified over three-fifths of the population gain from natural increase in Sweden. Disheartening conditions in Sweden's agriculture, class distinctions, and obligatory military service pushed her people out, while America's industrialization and her democratic way of life pulled them to her.

In 1880, the "New Norway" extended from Lake Michigan westward into the Dakotas and on toward the Missouri

River, and lay roughly, north of a line from Chicago westward to Sioux City.

1880

The Norwegian Grand Forks Tidende was established in Dakota in 1880, and there were enough Norwegians already living in the territory to make this newspaper a paying venture.

Beginning in 1880 and continuing for the next ten years, many of the 20 to 30,000 Norwegians arriving in America each year went directly to the new frontier in the Pacific Northwest.

January   There were already over 20,000 people of Norwegian stock settled in the Dakota Territory, most of them concentrated in the eastern counties.

Under the direction of W. W. Thomas, 787 Swedish immigrants had been settled in the Aroostook potatoe district of Maine. By 1900, Swedish born Maine residents numbered 2,247.

By 1880, the newspapers at Caribou, Maine, regularly printed one column in Swedish in a continuing effort to attract Swedish immigrants.

February   The Dannevirke, a Danish newspaper published at Cedar Falls, Iowa, became the official organ of the Danish Lutheran Church.

May   The first electric lights used in Chicago were installed in the store of Christian Jevne, a Norwegian who had come to that city in 1864. The Jevne store attracted street crowds night after night to witness the illumination.

October   A Norwegian sailor, Andrew Furuseth, emigrated to California. He was to become one of America's greatest labor leaders, and in 1895 he founded the International Seamen's Union.

November 2 Scandinavian-Americans as of 1880 had not completely broken with the Republican Party, and a good many of them voted for James A. Garfield for president. However, large blocs deserted to either the Democrats or the Greenback-Labor Party who had nominated James B. Weaver of Iowa for the presidency.

1881

Hans Mattson was appointed consul-general to India by President James A. Garfield.

Two Swedish immigrant guide books were published in Stockholm for prospective settlers; Hugo Risbeth's Emigrantens Vän and J. Bojeson's Till Amerika.

Beginning in 1881 and continuing for the next forty years, about 160,000 Swedes returned to their homeland out of the 880,000 who had emigrated to the United States by this time.

1882

This was the peak year of Norwegian emigration, when more than 29,000 Norwegians left their homeland for America. This was also the peak year for Swedish emigration when 64,607 persons arrived in the United States. The rugged climate of Minnesota and the Dakotas appealed to the bulk of these sturdy farmers, although many went to Michigan, Iowa, Indiana, Wisconsin, Illinois, and Oregon. However, Minnesota and the Dakotas were their principal destinations and by 1890, 400 Minnesota towns bore Swedish names, while travelers in Eastern Dakota reported that anyone speaking Norwegian could find companianship sooner than one whose sole language was English.

March — The first Danish fraternal organization, "The Danish Brotherhood," was organized in Omaha, Nebraska. By 1930, it had 15,139 members in 253 lodges.

June — In the early summer a caravan of forty wagons pulled by oxen left Minnesota carrying several hundred Norwegian immigrants into the eastern region of Dakota. Their choice of homes was largely determined by the waters of the Missouri River.

The high watermark of Danish immigration was reached in 1882, when 11,000 Danes arrived in a single year.

Most of the immigrants who came from Denmark were small farmers and laborers who sought land and jobs in the interior areas of America.

1883

Although Scandinavians in small numbers had been in Montana since the early 1870's, Norwegians and Swedes began moving into this state in large numbers in 1883.   A considerable amount settled on the grazing uplands of the Crazy Mountains, the Big Belt and the Little Belt Mountains, and the Flathead Mountains.

Anton M. Holter, who had moved to Montana in 1863, and had become one of the states leading pioneers, introduced a German machine for concentrating ores into the Montana mining industry.   Although he made a fortune in mining, Holter is most remembered as a great lumber baron.

October 22   The first prima donna of the New York Metropolitan Opera was a Swedish girl from Smaland, Christina Nilsson who dedicated this famous palace of song by singing Marguerite in Faust.   There have been many other Scandinavian opera stars from time to time.

1884

May   The Danish State Church decided to establish religious colonies in the United States.   In the succeeding years, it was very active and quite successful in scattering more than a dozen of these settlements throughout the northwest.

1885

April 9   The Federal government enacted a law which put an end to all forms of contract labor, thus terminating one way in which Swedish emigrants had been coming to the United States.

April 11   Thomas F. Bayard, a descendent of one of the original seventeenth century Swedish settlers was appointed Secretary of State by President Grover Cleveland.   He was the first Scandinavian-American to serve in a presidential cabinet.

June   An invitation was extended by the residents of Lincoln County, Minnesota, to the Danish State Church to establish a settlement in this rich farming area.

1886

The United Scandinavian Singers of America was organized but split on the rocks of Swedish, Norwegian, and Danish antagonism after having given three singing festivals.

Early in 1886, a Danish congregation was established in Lincoln County, Minnesota, and the Danes of this community built themselves a Folk High School even before they erected a church. The school was located at Tyler, Minnesota. Other church colonies were soon set up at Dannevang, Texas, Askov, Minnesota, Dagmar, Montana, Solveng, California, Kenmore, North Dakota, and Eugene, Oregon.

May 5

Mass meetings of Scandinavians in Chicago condemned the Haymarket Square Riot, and called those who had thrown the bombs, "traitors who had cast an ill-deserved repute on all foreign born." Many of these Scandinavians joined nativist associations in opposition to the emigration of new peoples from Southern and Eastern Europe.

November

Thousands of Scandinavian farmers in Minnesota and the Dakotas left the fold of the Republican Party, and joined the Farmer's Alliance which eventually became part of the Populist Party. This was quite a reversal on their part, for only ten years earlier they had refused to join the Granger Movement because of its secretive nature. But, agrarian distress in the mid-west was sharply mounting, and Scandinavians saw the only solution to their problems in political action.

1887

Although the state of Minnesota had a number of Norwegian newspapers, the largest was the Minnesota Tidende, founded in 1887 in Minneapolis by Thorwald Gulbrandson.

Hundreds of Norwegians went to work in the copper and iron mines of the Lake Superior district.

The first "Danish Folk Society" was established. Its founder and sponsor was Frederick Lange Grundtvig, and its basic purpose was the preservation of the cultural heritage of the Old World.

Swedish immigrants sent back to their homeland more than $3,000,000. By 1925, this figure had tripled.

June

Many Norwegian laborers were employed building the Great Northern Railroad owned by James J. Hill. When the railroad's tracks crossed the Dakota line into Montana, many of the Norwegians stayed on, taking up homesteads in the Great Falls region, working in the silver mines to the south, and finding jobs in the coal mines at Sand Coulee.

1888

The Norwegian Synod claimed that the public schools of the United States had low educational standards, and it made a strenuous attempt to dominate the policies of the school districts in which they had strong membership. They failed to do so.

Following the great exodus of 1882, the second highest year of Swedish emigration to the United States was 1888, when almost 55,000 persons departed the Old Country for the New World.

Swedish-Americans became the first of the farming population in the United States to adopt electric lights on their farms and in their homes.

August   The Swedes, Danes, and Norwegians, accustomed to popular education in their homelands, gave hearty support to better schools in the United States. The language question, however, caused trouble, particularly among the more recent Scandinavian arrivals. In Dakota Territory, they openly defied the law, requiring the teaching of English. In Wisconsin and Illinois, the Scandinavians successfully united with other ethnic groups to force through the repeal of state laws which refused to recognize schools in which English was not the language of instruction.

November 6   Although many Scandinavians throughout the mid-west cast their votes for Grover Cleveland and the Democrats, Benjamin Harrison and the Republicans won the election. The 1888 election was an indication of growing Scandinavian-American disaffection with the Republican Party.

1889

The Freja Society consolidated with the Swedish Singing Society of Chicago to form the <u>Svenska Gleeklubben</u>, an organization that won many prizes in competitive singing.

The largest chair factory in the United States was established by a Norwegian immigrant in Chicago.

Because of the flight to the cities during the 1880's, the state of Vermont, in attempting to stem the rural exodus, tried the expedient of colonizing three small groups of Swedish immigrants on deserted tracts of land. Although some of the Swedes remained in these areas, the project was basically a failure.

Perth Amboy, New Jersey, just outside of New York City, and the major port of entry for the Danes, attracted a large group of Danish immigrants chiefly because of the great terra cotta works located there, which were owned by two earlier Danish immigrants, Albert Mathissen, and Eric Eskensen and their families.

November 5   Anton M. Holter was elected to the Montana State Legislature, the first Norwegian so honored in that state.

1890

The census reported that 88,132 Danes had arrived in the United States during the 1880's forming the peak years of Danish emigration.

Scandinavian seamen continued to desert their ships anchored in American ports. By 1890, the total had reached an astonishing 34,000.

The Texas State Census indicated that 1,300 persons of Norwegian ancestry and 700 of Swedish background lived in the state. However, the attraction of the South was never very strong in Scandinavia.

According to the census, the city of Minneapolis had replaced Chicago as the main urban destination of Scandinavians coming to the United States.

1890

When the census of 1890 was taken, it showed that Norwegians were the most numerous foreign born element in the Dakotas; North Dakota having almost 50,000 Norwegians, and South Dakota over 35,000. The Norwegians had pioneered the desirable agricultural area in the eastern two-thirds of North Dakota.

The Augustana Synod under Hasselquist's direction had grown to 325 pastors, 637 congregations and 84,583 communicants by 1890.

January   Through the efforts of men such as Hans Mattson, Jay Cooke, President of the Northern Pacific Railroad, and James J. Hill of the Great Northern Railroad, a continuous Scandinavian agricultural district extending hundreds of miles, and dotted with farms, villages and towns, had been established from Minnesota through Montana. While Hill did perform magnificent work in settling these regions, there is no doubt that his "empire" was one of the causes behind the rise of agrarian radicalism among the Scandinavians in these areas.

April Jacob A. Riis, undoubtedly the most well-known Danish-American, published his important book, How the Other Half Lives. This work, and others, succeeded in arousing the social conscience of New York City to improve life in the slums and among the poor.

November Scandinavians in the mid-west supported candidates backed by the Farmer's Alliances. They were instrumental in getting a number of their candidates elected to the House of Representatives, and were beginning to move toward the program of bimet⁺alism advocated by "free silver" groups.

December An article which appeared in a national magazine reported that cheerlessness and hardships of farm life in the mid and upper mid-west accounted for an uncommonly high proportion of insanity among the Norwegian and Swedish immigrant farm settlers.

1891

In 1891, the character of Danish immigration changed, and more skilled artisans and professional men came to the United States than did farmers and laborers.

From 1882 to 1891, Danish immigration did not exceed 10,000 arrivals. In 1891, however, 10,600 Danes came to the United States.

1891

Norwegian emigration, beginning in 1891, dropped to 5,000 to 6,000 annually, while Swedish emigration declined to 7,000 to 8,000 per year.

In reply to a questionaire sent to the governors of states by the Immigration Restriction League, twelve state governments expressed a desire for immigrants of Scandinavian backgrounds. That they were hard working, god fearing and non-radical, were the reasons running through most of the replies.

September Reindeer were brought to Alaska from Siberia and from Norway to provide a domestic industry for the dwindling Eskimo tribes. A young Norwegian, William A. Kjellman of Wisconsin, supervised and instructed the Eskimos in the care of the animals. Inevitably, too, Alaskan fishing waters drew permanent Norwegian and Swedish settlers to the northern outpost of America. One of the earliest Norwegians who came to Alaska was Peter Thoms Buschmann, who developed the salmon fishing and canning industry in that future state.

1892

Andrew Jenson, the leading independent leaf tobacco producer in Wisconsin, served as a presidential elector in 1892, and was a candidate for state treasurer on the Democratic ticket in 1906.

By 1892, the Danish Church in America had 56 ministers, many parochial schools, an immigrant mission in New York City, a theological school at West Denmark, Wisconsin, and an orphanage in Chicago.

By the beginning of 1892, 70,000 Scandinavians were working in Chicago, the men as mechanics or factory hands, the women usually as domestic servants. Scandinavians in the Twin-Cities of Minneapolis and St. Paul numbered more than 50,000 with new accretions being added daily.

November 8   The Democratic party made some inroads on the Swedish Republican vote; it advertised heavily in Swedish newspapers and financed several new publications. A dozen Swedish journals deserted their old political allies, largely because of the unpopularity of the McKinley Tariff of 1890 and the alleged flirtation of the party leaders with the saloon interests.

The election of Knute Nelson as Governor of Minnesota denoted the political coming of age of Norwegian-Americans. He was the first Norwegian-American governor in the United States, after having been elected to Congress for three terms beginning in 1883.

1892

Much to the dismay of the Populists, Scandinavians voted against Populist Party candidates in both the state and national elections, despite the efforts of orators and newspaper editors to gain their adherence, and despite the fact that they came primarily from the states where Populism was the strongest. Although Populism was strong in some Scandinavian areas, as a group, they apparently reversed their earlier movement toward agrarian radicalism. The reasons for this change are complex and often quite obscure.

1893

The "Danish Sisterhood," a fraternal organization was established. By 1930, it had 7,000 members in 143 lodges located mainly in states of the mid-west.

Much proselyting was done by non-Lutheran Protestants in the early Danish settlements and dissension broke out among the Danes themselves over theological questions such as affiliating with other Scandinavian Lutheran synods.

At the World's Fair in Chicago, the American Union of Swedish Singers gave concerts with a chorus of 500, assisted by artists from Sweden and the Theodore Thomas Orchestra.

April   The Columbian Exposition to be held in Chicago during the summer drew hundreds of Norwegians to the city, where they found work in building the fair as carpenters, masons, and laborers.

May 5   A severe panic struck the nation. It caused severe hardships among Scandinavian-American farmers of the mid-west, many of whom lost heavily as a result of their mortgaged land. Thousands of them pushed onward to the Pacific frontier settling in Northern California, Washington and Oregon. Many of those who remained, lost faith in the major political parties once more, and began to drift into the Populist ranks again.

September   Once they had left the Old Country, Swedish immigrants were given little or no attention by the established church in Sweden. It was not until 1893, that a Swedish State-Church Bishop visited the various Swedish communities in America.

1894

The Danish People's Society, which was organized to preserve the religion and national customs of the Danes, established three Danish farming and dairying communities from 1894 to 1919.

1894

Like the Norwegians, Swedish-Americans performed a great and valuable amount of work in railroad construction in the mid and far west. They were especially helpful in building the Great Northern Railroad, and James J. Hill, its president, said in 1894, "Give me Swedes, snuff and whiskey, and I'll build a railroad through hell."

March 25   Several small detachments of unemployed Scandinavian-Americans started out to join "Coxey's Army," led by the populist Jacob S. Coxey of Ohio in its march on Washington, D. C. As conditions worsened in the middle-west during the depression following the Panic of 1893, Scandinavian-Americans, especially Norwegians, began backing Populist candidates once again.

July   With the mounting influx of new immigrants from Southern and Eastern Europe, Scandinavian-Americans, in some areas of the mid-west, joined a new nativist organization, the American Protective Association, whose program of anti-Catholicism was quite appealing. So many Scandinavians joined the A. P. A. that the A. P. A. journal in Minneapolis merged with a leading Scandinavian newspaper in that city.

November 5 The Populist Party registered a number of victories in the Congressional elections of 1894, especially in heavily Scandinavian populated states such as North and South Dakota, Minnesota and Wisconsin.

1895

By 1895, two Norwegian newspapers were opened in Crookston, North Dakota, indicating that the "Great Dakota Boom," had attracted a goodly amount of Scandinavians.

Eighteen Norwegian born residents of Minneapolis, who had long felt the need for a society for mutual aid, organized the Sons of Norway, the largest and most active of the Norwegian secular organizations in America.

November 3 Knute Nelson became the first Norwegian-American to be elected to the United States Senate. He was successively elected to five terms in the Senate, dying in office in 1923, at the age of eighty.

December   After their short whirl within the ranks of the A. P. A.
many Scandinavians lost sympathy with this nativist organization as its anti-foreign tinge, in addition to its anti-
Catholic tinge, became increasingly emphatic; in Minnesota, the hotbed of A. P. A. activity among Scandinavians,
the order lost most of its members of Norse origins.

Clifton College was founded by Norwegians in Texas.   It
was sponsored by the Norwegian Lutheran Church, and
was co-educational from its inception.

1896

In 1896, the United Danish Evangelical Lutheran Church of
America was organized, and it became the largest Danish
church body in the United States.

Ole Edvart Rölvaag came to the United States and settled
on an uncle's farm in South Dakota.   His experiences of
pioneering in South Dakota, as well as the experiences and
stories of his wife's family (Jennie Berdahl Rölvaag) furnished the material that was to become part of his classic
in American literature, Giants in the Earth.

Julegraven, an illustrated Christmas magazine written in
Danish began operations in Cedar Falls, Iowa.   In 1920,
at Blair, Nebraska, another magazine of this type, but
published in English, became popular with Danish-Americans.

November 3   In the campaign of 1896, the Swedish bureau of the Republican National Committee in Chicago left no stone unturned
to hold the Swedish voters for William McKinley.   It sent
out over 7,000 letters, nearly 800,000 books in Swedish,
and 700,000 copies of Swedish newspapers.

Despite their Populist leanings, most Scandinavians cast
their ballots for William McKinley and against William
Jennings Bryan and Populism.   Improved economic conditions, their customary conservatism, and the influence of
the Scandinavian churches, who raised an almost unanimous
voice against the Populists and their "political heresies,"
caused the Scandinavians to vote Republican once more.
Although most Scandinavians did not vote for Bryan, the
Norwegians of South Dakota were mostly pro-Populist.

Two Norwegian newspapers, Normanden (Grand Forks, North Dakota), edited by a well-known writer, H. A. Foss, and Nye Normanden (Moorhead, Minnesota), reflected the Populist sympathies of the Norwegian farmers of the Red River Valley during this period. In 1896, the first governor of South Dakota with a Norwegian background, Andrew E. Lee, was elected. He was an ardent populist.

1898

The Kensington Stone, a slab with Runic inscriptions and dated 1362 was found in Minnesota. The stone, originally pronounced a forgery, showed that Norsemen penetrated America as far west as Minnesota. Its case has recently been revised by the Scandinavian-American scholar, H. R. Holand.

November 4   John Lind became the first Swedish American to be elected governor of a state. Running on the Republican ticket in Minnesota, he easily defeated his Democratic opponent.

December   In the winter of 1898, Jafet Lindeberg, a Norwegian reindeer herder, came to Alaska with a herd that had been purchased by the American government in Norway. Instead of herding reindeer, he began to pan for gold in the Snake River and struck a rich vein. In 90 days he took out $200,000 worth of gold, and helped found the town of Nome, Alaska. He became the president of the Pioneer Mining Company and by the time of the First World War, was the richest Norwegian in America.

1899

November 6   One of the best known members of the House of Representatives was the Norwegian Gilbert N. Haugen, a Republican from Iowa, who served from 1899 to 1933. His activities, as one might expect, centered on the agricultural program, the McNary-Haugen Bill of 1924 receiving most public notice.

1900

At the turn of the century, Scandinavians were still emigrating to the United States in fairly large numbers. For example, beginning in 1900 and extending to 1910, 65,285 Danes arrived in America, while 190,505 Norwegians, and 249,534 Swedes took residence in the United States as well.

By 1900, the Scandinavians were sufficiently numerous in Minneapolis to overshadow other immigrant groups. They played an active role in the city, and made it, in effect, the Scandinavian capital of America, the center of Swedish and Norwegian papers, churches and seminaries.

The greater bulk of Norwegian immigration was moving into the Pacific Northwest, (Washington and Oregon) after the depression of the 1890's had worn off.

Hundreds of Swedes settled in areas north of Cape Cod, Massachusetts, but not in great enough numbers to dominate the area or any one activity. The majority, however continued to go to the traditional areas of Swedish settlement, the middle west.

As early as 1900, it was found that Swedish was beginning to decline in Swedish colleges, both for lecturing and religious services, though pastors were still required to know the old language when appointed.

1900

In Kansas, Swedish dominated the church scene until the end of the eighteenth century. English was used in the public schools, but Swedish Lutherans organized summer schools using the language of the old country.

By 1900 there were 400 places in Minnesota that bore Swedish names, and whole townships were peopled by this Scandinavian nationality.

By 1900, when the Populists failed to bring the reforms the Norwegian farmers had hoped for, and when rising wheat prices brought a measure of prosperity again, most of the Dakota-Minnesota Norwegians reentered the Republican Party.

Beginning in 1900 and extending into the first two decades of the twentieth century, the great reform movement known as Progressivism captured the imagination and support of the majority of Scandinavian-Americans. Many of them actively participated in the movement. Local and state officials, governors, congressmen and senators of Norwegian and Swedish backgrounds were elected and reelected during these years. Some of the most famous of these Scandinavian Progressives were Ernest Lundeen of Minnesota, Eskil C. Carlson of Iowa, Oscar Carlstrom of Illinois, and Floyd Björnstjerne Olson of Minnesota.

November 6   The real turn toward Progressivism and liberalism came
when the first generation of American-born Scandinavians
reached adult years.   They showed this when they backed
Robert M. LaFollette in Wisconsin in his election to governor and during his subsequent terms in the state house and
in the Senate.

1902

Scandinavian emigration from 1902 to 1910 rose to high
points of from 40,000 to 45,000 a year.   After 1910, it
levelled off, dropped during the First World War, and
increased ever so slightly in the few years before the
quota system was established in the United States.

The Danes, as a group, favored the Progressive movement,
although they provided no outstanding leaders or made any
lasting contributions.

Ernst Frederik Verner Alexanderson, born in Uppsala,
came to the United States in 1902.   He became chief engineer for the Radio Corporation of America, and worked out
the modern selector receiver for radios.

Three expert glass blowers from Norway started a minor
stream of these skilled artisans, from the noted glasswork
centers in Norway, to Corning, New York, which rapidly
became a major producer of glass products in the United
States.

1905

Minnesota, the most Scandinavian state in the Union had a
population of 1,997,401 of which 223,000 had been born in
Sweden, and 111,000 had been born in Norway.   The per-
centages of Swedish and Norwegian foreign stock were much
higher.

1906

By 1906, there were 40,000 Swedes in Texas, scattered
throughout the state in a number of fairly homogeneous Swedish areas.

1907

In 1907, the Mormon Church of Utah had almost seventy
missionaries in Sweden.

1909

In 1909, the Mormons claimed over 17,000 converts in Sweden, of whom nearly 8,000--------mostly young unmarried
women and skilled artisans attracted by the high wages
prevailing in Utah---came to the United States.

Ole Evinrude, a Norwegian-American, invented the out-
board boat motor, and became the president of a $4,000,000
corporation which manufactured half of the nation's out-
board motors by 1929.

1910

The census of 1910 revealed that of all Norwegians in
America as of this date only 10 percent were laborers,
while out of all Swedes in the country 13 percent were
common laborers.

By 1910, the highest peak of Swedish, Norwegian, and Danish
born population had been reached. The figures were respectively 1,021,165; 665,189; and 258,053. From 1910
on the totals for each group declined.

Even as late as 1910, Scandinavian immigrants were less
inclined to settle in cities than other immigrant arrivals.
A good example, was the fact that out of the 100,000 first
and second generation, Scandinavian-Americans that went
to the Dakotas during the first decade of the twentieth century, only five percent settled in cities. On the other hand
most of the new Scandinavians who came to Washington and
Oregon became urban rather than rural dwellers.

November 5   Beginning in 1910, the Republican Party, in order to cement
the hold over mid-western politics and the Scandinavian
vote, began actively nominating Swedes and Norwegians
for a variety of offices. In that year, a Swede, Adolph Olson Eberhart, became the Republican governor of Minnesota.

THE END OF SCANDINAVIAN IMMIGRATION
(1911-1950)

1911

In the decade from 1911 to 1920, Scandinavian emigration
to the United States considerably declined. Throughout
the entire period, totals of 95,074 Swedes, 66,395 Norwegians, and 41,983 Danes came to America. These figures

represented decreases of 154,460 Swedes, 124,110 Norwegians, and 23,302 Danes who had come to the United States during the previous decade.

1912

November 5   In the Republican split between President William Howard Taft and ex-President Theodore Roosevelt in the election of 1912, most Swedish-born voters, especially those of the midwest, backed the Bull-Moose Party of Roosevelt. The Norwegians, who had supported Robert La Follette Sr. in his insurgency from Republican ranks, were inclined to return to the Republican fold on election day.

1913

Like the other Scandinavian groups, the Danes founded and supported their own societies and lodges. The United Danish Societies of America were incorporated in 1913 to provide cooperative life insurance and certain social advantages.

Gideon Sundbäck, born in Sweden, provided the present generation with the zipper fastener, which he perfected in 1913.

1914

By 1914, the state of Wisconsin held the greatest number of Norwegians living in the United States. They were scattered throughout every corner of the state, but the largest concentrations of them could be found in the south-central part, with Dane County as a center.

1914

June 28   When war broke out in Europe, opinion among Scandinavian-Americans was somewhat divided. At first, the Swedes were, generally, pro-German. It was difficult, if not impossible, to convince a Swedish-American, familiar with the history of his native land, that Russia was fighting in the interests of Democracy and for the rights of smaller nations. The Swedish-American clergy, whose influence counted heavily, were strongly pro-German. The Norwegians were more evenly divided, but the majority were pro-ally, while the Danes with the background of the Schleswig-Holstein War, were violently anti-German.

World War I in Europe, seriously reduced Scandinavian emigration to the United States, very few coming to America between 1914 and 1918. The numbers would increase slightly during the last two years of the decade.

September   Knute Rockne, one of the most famous Norwegian-American figures in the world of sports, became the football coach at the University of Notre Dame in South Bend, Indiana. He had come to the United States from Voss, Norway as a small boy, and with his family settled in Chicago. As a coach, he was an innovator, and a symbol of sportsmanship.

1915

By 1915, Norwegian emigration to the United States totaled over 750,000, a figure larger than four-fifths of the entire population of Norway at the beginning of the nineteenth century.

Andrew Furuseth, the great Norwegian-American labor leader, was instrumental in aiding Robert La Follette in the passage of a major piece of reform legislation, the La Follette Seamen's Act. Furuseth, President of the International Seamen's Union, along with three other Norwegians---John P. Hansen, P. H. Olsen, and Peter B. Gill, and a Swede, Oscar Baldwin, were primarily responsible for the writing of this Act.

After the sailing vessels had had their day, there was little direct Swedish passenger traffic to New York until 1915, when the Swedish-American line was organized. Within ten years after that, the new American quota law had reduced Swedish emigration to a fraction of what it had been formerly.

July   Scandinavian-Americans formed the backbone of the Farmer's Non-Partisan League, which invited Democrats and Republicans to discard their outworn political programs and make a more fundamental attack upon the difficulties that beset farmers. In time, the League expanded into the Farmer-Labor Party of the northwest. Its program grew more revolutionary, as it attempted to cope with the larger economic issues under such leaders as Floyd B. Olson, the Norwegian who would occupy the governor's chair in Minnesota.

1916

November 7   The Scandinavian-Americans were split in their choice of a President in the election of 1916. In general, the Norwegians voted for the Republican candidate, Charles Evans

Hughes, while the Danes and especially the Swedes gave their votes to the incumbent Woodrow Wilson.

1917

By 1917, the "college mania" that had been sweeping through the Swedish-American element had subsided. Swedish enthusiasm for the establishment of institutions of higher learning was unmatched by any other immigrant group in the United States.

In 1917, after prolonged negotiations, the Norwegian Synod, the Norwegian United Church, and Hauge's Synod banded together as the Norwegian Lutheran Church of America.

The Scandinavian-Americans contributed more to the development of lumbering in Montana than any other national group. The Gyppo Contract System, commonly used in Montana's lumber camps, was introduced largely to satisfy their demands after the 1917 general strike of lumbermen in that state.

By 1917, there had been, since 1825, 450 newspapers and periodicals in the Norwegian language, an overwhelming proportion of them lasting less than five years. This number included religious as well as secular journals.

January 17　　The United States purchased the Danish West Indies (Virgin Islands) from Denmark for $25,000,000. The inhabitants, mainly Negroes, but also about 3,200 Danes were not given American citizenship until 1927.

April 6　　With the declaration of war against Germany, Scandinavian-Americans solidly backed their country against the enemy, and enlisted in the armed forces in large numbers.

December 18　The Danes, backed by the Danish language press opposed the passage of the Prohibition Amendment.

1918

By the end of the First World War, Swedish immigration dropped to a few thousand annually. The great waves from Sweden had run their course as early as 1910, but Swedes continued to come to the United States in diminished numbers. In 1918, less than 2,500 Swedes emigrated. Comparable statistics applied to the Norwegians and Danes.

In 1918, in the twelve states where most of the Norwegians lived, there were 19 Lutheran colleges and professional schools and numerous academies.

July 4 The Swedish-Lutheran Church resolved officially that the immigrants and their children ought to learn English, the language of their new country, but that Swedish ought to be preserved as a rich cultural inheritance as long as possible.

1919

October 28 Andrew Volstead, a Norwegian Congressman from Minnesota, wrote the law that brought the United States the speakeasy, bootleggers, and bathtub gin.

1920

The census reported that there were approximately 190,000 people in the United States who were born in Denmark. In addition, there were 277,415 born in the United States of Danish parentage, thus making a total of about 467,000 of Danish stock. Of this number, Iowa had the largest and Minnesota the second largest group, but in neither state did the total reach 50,000.

The decade of the twenties saw a sharp reduction in Scandinavian emigration to the United States. In this ten year period, Swedish emigration dropped to 97,249, Danish emigration to 32,430, and Norwegian emigration to 68,531. The last major influxes came in the few years before the quota law went into effect.

As late as 1920, over 17,000 inhabitants of Iowa were born in Norway. In the same year, Minnesota had a population of over 90,000 who were born in Norway. The greatest concentration of Norwegians in this state was in the southeastern portion.

Scandinavian immigration during the twenties also saw the number of Scandinavian-born residents increase in the industrial states of Connecticut, Massachusetts, New York, Michigan, Illinois and Pennsylvania, and decline considerably in the agricultural states of Iowa, Wisconsin, Minnesota, Montana and North and South Dakota. The largest increases of Scandinavian population were recorded in Washington, Oregon, and especially California.

1920

Following their brief interlude with nativism in the 1890's, Scandinavians once again showed their undiluted "Americanism," by joining in the cry for higher bars against the "new immigration" coming from Southern and Eastern Europe.

Mary Anderson, a Swedish immigrant who came to Montana in the 1890's, was appointed the head of the Woman's Bureau of the Department of Labor by President Woodrow Wilson.

As in Sweden, Norwegian emigrants were urged to return to their native land, and apply techniques learned in America. In time many did return, the majority settling in rural areas in the Old Country. By 1920, some 50,000 Norwegian-Americans returned to Norway.

The Danish Brotherhood was a secret society that developed from an organization of Danish World War I veterans.

August 26   The Danes, supported by the Danish-language newspapers came out in opposition to the passage of the Woman's Suffrage Amendment.

November 2   When the Farmer-Labor Party succeeded the Republican Party in many sections of the mid-west, large numbers of Swedish-Americans supported its nominees, including P.P. Christansen, a Dane from Utah, who ran for the Presidency.

1921

As late as 1921, 85 percent of the preaching of the Swedish-Lutheran Church was in Swedish. However, the effect of World War I, and the post-war agitation against foreign language, religious services hastened the transition to English.

Since 1921, there have been several Dakota governors of Norwegian birth or descent, all of them Republicans. Among them were John Moses, and Fred Aandahl.

In 1921, 73 of the 86 counties of Minnesota had one or more Swedish office-holders.

May 19   Congress passed the Emergency Quota Law, which ended the era of unrestricted immigration. Under this first quota, 6000 Danes, 9,000 Norwegians, and 11,000 Swedes were permitted to enter the United States annually.

June 2   The Swedish-Lutheran Church in America officially re-
                solved to begin conducting all services in English.

November 4   Jacob Preus became the second governor of Norwegian
                descent in the state of Minnesota. Since that time, at
                least a half dozen chief executives of that state have been
                of part or full Norwegian stock.

1922

In 1922, the Danish Sisterhood had 8,000 members in 145
lodges. Like other Danish societies it made an effort
to keep alive the memories of the mother country and to
emphasize the Danish cultural heritage.

1923

Kristian Prestgard became the editor of the Decorah
Posten. Until his death in 1946, he was perhaps the most
influential newspaper editor among Norwegian-Americans.

A Swedish archbishop dedicated the new seminary buildings
at Rock Island, Illinois, and in 1926 the college received a
visit from the Swedish Crown Prince.

1924

After the First World War, Sweden suffered from a serious
economic depression, while the United States enjoyed a
boom. As a result, there was a revival of Swedish emigration just before the new quota law went into effect, and the
number of Swedes entering the United States in 1924 reached a post-war high of 18,310.

A Danish-Norwegian woman's magazine, printed in Cedar
Rapids, Iowa, and known as Kvinden og Hjemmet had a
circulation of over 26,000 in 1924.

May 26   The National Origins Act with discriminatory national and
                racial quotas was adopted. The total quota for Southern
                and Eastern European countries was set at 24,222; for
                Northern and Western Europe, 126,053; of which the Swe-
                dish quota was 3,313, the Norwegian quota, 2,337, and the
                Danish quota 2,189.

1925

It is estimated that by 1925, the Swedish immigrant farmers
had cleared or farmed over 12,000,000 acres of land in the
United States.

The Augustana Synod owned property estimated at over $31,000,000, of which nearly $900,000 was invested in immigrant homes.

The National Ski Association, organized by Norwegians in 1904, had 20,000 members. National tournaments had been arranged since 1916.

1925

As late as 1925, Chicago had nearly 50,000 inhabitants of Norwegian blood.

June   The Norwegian-American Centennial was celebrated at St. Paul, Minnesota. The principal speaker was President Calvin Coolidge. The event coincided with the closing of the gates of immigration by the quota system, and for all intents and purposes, emigration from Norway came to a halt as compared with the past.

October 6   The Norwegian-American Historical Association was founded at Northfield, Minnesota, with Theodore C. Blegen as managing editor of the Association's publications.

November 5   Unlike Norwegians in other middle-western states, those of Montana became Democrats. The first Norwegian-American governor to be elected in Montana was John E. Erickson, who served from 1925 to 1933.

1926

Carl Sandburg, the most eminent American author of Swedish descent, was of parents who came to Illinois from Sweden in the 1870's. In 1926, his monumental biography of Abraham Lincoln began to appear.

As late as 1926, the very isolated Danish community of Askov, Minnesota, was still using much Danish language in its schools.

1927

May 21   Colonel Charles A. Lindberg Jr., a son of a Swedish immigrant who rose to high political office in the United States, made his famous pioneer flight, New York non-stop to Paris, and instituted a new era in American aviation. He, more than any other man popularized this new means of transportation.

1928

November 6   With the exception of a few isolated Democratic strongholds in Montana, South Dakota, Chicago, and St. Paul, Scandinavian-Americans voted overwhelmingly for Herbert Hoover in the Presidential election.

1929

The Leif Erikson Memorial Association of America, to promote the establishment of a Leif Erikson Day was organized.

July 1   The National Origins Act of 1929 further reduced the quotas of Scandinavian emigrants to the United States to less than one thousand for Danes, Swedes, and Norwegians.

November   Leonard Seppala, a Norwegian-American, placed the markers in the ice bound wastes of the South Pole to guide the flyers of the Admiral Richard Byrd expedition to their landing places.

1930

In 1930, there were still 43 Swedish newspapers published in the United States according to Ayer's Newspaper Annual and Directory.

By 1930, there were 5,000 Norwegians in Wayne County, Michigan, as many Danes, and about 13,500 Swedes, most of whom lived in Detroit and its immediate vicinity. They had been attracted to Michigan by the opportunities in the automobile industry.

With the quota system limiting foreign emigration to America, the decade of the 1930's saw a minute fraction of Scandinavians arrive in America as compared to pre-quota days. Only 2,559 Danes, 4,740 Norwegians, and 3,960 Swedes emigrated to the United States during this entire ten year period.

The census of 1930 showed that Minnesota had 267,953 Norwegian immigrants or children of immigrants; Wisconsin and North Dakota had approximately 125,000 each, with Washington, New York and Illinois each with approximately 75,000. The tendency on the part of Norwegians to avoid congregation in large cities was evidenced by the fact that there were only four cities of more than 100,000 in which there were more than 5,000 Norwegians; New

York, 38,130; Chicago, 21,740, Minneapolis, 15,592, and Seattle, 9,745. On the other hand, there was a greater tendency among second generation Swedes to settle in cities rather than the rural areas.

The census also revealed that, by 1930, the Twin Cities of Minneapolis and St. Paul attracted the majority of Scandinavians who went to the cities of the mid-west. However, of all the Swedes who lived in America at that time, 80 percent still lived in rural districts.

1931

The great Notre Dame football coach, Knute Rockne, was killed in an airplane crash. The tributes paid to his memory exceeded anything known in the history of athletics. King Haakon of Norway ordered the Norwegian consul at Chicago to attend the funeral at South Bend with a delegation of Norwegians.

1932

Census returns indicated a continual drift of Danish-Americans from their original rural regions in the United States to the cities of America by 1932.

In 1932, there were five Norwegian and two Swedish Congressmen elected from the state of Minnesota.

November 8   By 1932, Scandinavians, as a group, had established a working alliance with Franklin Delano Roosevelt's leadership of the Democratic Party, although they successfully maintained an independent position. Although they went overwhelmingly for Roosevelt in 1932, their independence made them the most dynamic immigrant factor in the realignment of American political parties during the 1930's.

1933

In 1933, when Sweden had recovered from the "Great Depression" more than the United States, only 105 Swedes entered the country, and as late as 1935, only 160.

1934

June   The centennial of the founding of Fox River colony in La Salle County, Illinois was celebrated. A monument to Cleng Peerson was erected and dedicated.

1935

President Franklin Delano Roosevelt asked Congress to proclaim October 9 Leif Erikson Day, throughout the land, that date being chosen because it was on October 9, 1825 that the first modern day Norwegians arrived in the United States.

Max Henius, a Danish immigrant and a noted chemist, probably trained more brewmasters in the United States than any other person, through the influence of the Wahl-Henius Chemical Laboratory and Brewing Institute of Chicago.

From 1935 to the outbreak of World War II, Sweden enjoyed full employment with increasingly improved wages and social security benefits, and at no time during these years was the Swedish immigration quota of 1924 even approximately filled.

August 14   The Scandinavian American press, in general, applauded the passage of the Social Security Act.

1936

Luther College became coeducational.

The Norwegian-Lutheran Church in America voted to drop the word Norwegian from its name.

Minnesota's very able governor of Norwegian ancestry, Floyd Bjornstjerne Olson died. He had been elected in 1930 on the Farmer-Labor ticket. His death at the age of 44 removed a very promising statesman from the national scene; one whom many predicted might have become President of the United States.

1938

By 1938, the number of Scandinavian newspapers being published in the United States had considerably declined. There were a total of 87;16 Danish, 29 Norwegian, and 42 Swedish. Although these newspapers could be found in most of the major cities of the country, their main regions of distribution were the upper mid-west and the Mississippi Valley.

A monument in black, Swedish granite, designed by the famous Swedish born sculptor, Carl Milles, and presented to the state of Delaware by the school children of Sweden, was erected on the spot where the first Swedes landed in America in 1638.

1940

In 1940, the Danish Brotherhood was no longer a secret society, and by this time it had a membership of 15,000.

In 1940, a village of nearly 300 people marked the site of Eric Janson's Bishop Hill Colony and some of the old buildings were left as mute testimony of its former prosperity.

During the entire decade of the 1940's, a slight upswing in Scandinavian emigration to the United States occurred, primarily as a result of World War II, and the dislocations following its conclusion. Danish emigrants during these years numbered 5,393, those from Norway, 10,100, and from Sweden, 10,665. Most of them entered the country in the post-1945 period under a presidential order facilitating the entry of displaced persons.

The census reported 97,000 Norwegian Americans in North Dakota, 42,000 in South Dakota, and 50,000 in Montana. Fifty percent of these persons still lived in rural communities.

As of 1940, only 8.2 percent of the total population of Minnesota was Scandinavian in origins. The common impression that Minnesota is a predominantly Scandinavian state may therefore be accepted as an unconscious tribute to the strong personal qualities of the people from the North.

1940

In fact, the Bay Ridge area of Brooklyn, New York, sometimes facetiously called a suburb of Oslo, in 1940, had the largest concentration of Norwegian-Americans outside of Norway; almost 55,000 persons.

California boasted a population of over 15,000 Norwegians, and about 26,000 Swedes, while the census reported that 3,646 inhabitants of Texas had been born in Sweden, with 7,900 listed as second generation with one or both parents born in Sweden. How many there were of later generations did not appear in this report.

Inevitably, the Alaskan fishing waters drew permanent Scandinavian settlers to this northern outpost of the United States. By 1940, there were 2,444 Norwegians and 1,500 Swedes living in this future state.

Swedes in Chicago numbered 46,258 making it the third largest Swedish city in the world. Their children born in America added up to 63,940. For the state of Illinois, the corresponding figures in 1940 were, respectively, 79,906 and 130,540.

November 5   Edwin Bergstrom, a Norwegian-American, was appointed chief consulting architect of the United States War Department, and as such was the chief designer of the Pentagon complex in Washington, D. C.

1941

December 7   With the bombing of Pearl Harbor, and the entry of the United States into World War II, Scandinavian-Americans again exhibited their patriotism. They joined the armed forces by the thousands and contributed in a variety of ways to the war effort. The chief American air ace in the Pacific theater of war was Major Richard I. Bong, whose father had been a Swedish immigrant in the 1880's.

No fewer than 88 percent of all Norwegian church services in the United States were being held in English rather than Norwegian.

1942

The distinguished archeologist, Philip Ainsworth Means, examined the whole question of a curious cylindrical tower still standing in Newport, Rhode Island, and believed to be a fourteenth century Viking structure, possibly the oldest Christian church in the entire western hemisphere.

In 1942, a Norse Battalion was formed as part of the Ninth Infantry Regiment and stationed at Fort Snelling. Trained for winter warfare to help in liberating Norway, the soldiers in this battalion were required to speak Norwegian reasonably well.

July   Colonel Evans Carlson, leader of the Marine battalion, known as Carlson's Raiders, was the grandson of one of a small band of forty niners who left Norway for the California gold fields. Colonel Carlson led the surprise attack on Makin Island in the Solomons, and his raider battalion fought gallantly at Guadalcanal.

Other noted World War II military figures of Scandinavian background were Major General Leif Sverdup who came to the United States in 1914, Colonel Roger O. Egeberg, a Norwegian whose father had been born in Norway, and the personal physician to General Douglas MacArthur throughout the war, and Lieutenant General Lauris Norstad, son of a Chicago Lutheran pastor, who later became head of all NATO forces in Europe.

1944

November 7   Franklin D. Roosevelt was elected for a fourth term. While many Scandinavian-Americans voted for him once more, strong inroads were made by Thomas E. Dewey and the Republican Party in several Scandinavian regions, especially in the rural middle-west.

1946

January   The first Swedish-American to be appointed to a post-war cabinet post was Clinton P. Anderson, of New Mexico, as Secretary of Agriculture. There have been several other cabinet posts held by Scandinavian-Americans since 1946.

1947

Finn Ronne, a Norwegian born explorer and engineer, led, under the auspices of the American Geographical Society, an expedition to the Antarctic, where he mapped the last unchartered coastline in the world. He definitely established that Antartica was one continent.

Henry O. Jaastad, a Norwegian-American, known as the perpetual mayor of Tuscon, Arizona, retired. In 18 years of conservative, but constructive administration, he made Tuscon into one of the model cities of the nation.

October   The Northern Wisconsin Co-operative Tobacco Pool, celebrated its twenty fifth anniversary. The membership of this organization was heavily Norwegian-American with George Nygaard as President, and M.T. Jenson as Vice-President.

1948

The Kensington Stone was placed in the Smithsonian Institute. Dr. Matthew W. Stirling, chief of the government's

Bureau of American Ethnology, called it "probably the most important archeological object yet found in North America."

The term "daughter church" was adopted to indicate the relation between the Swedish State Church and the Augustana Evangelical Lutheran Church, the primary church of Swedish-Americans of Lutheran persuasion.

Bernt Balchen, a Norwegian-American who had come to the United States in 1927, was recalled to active duty in the United States Air Force at his own request. An air hero in World War II, he was considered "the greatest pilot in the world, bar none."

May   The Arch-Bishop of Uppsala, Sweden, attended a Swedish Pioneer Centennial held at Minneapolis.

May 17   A report in the Nordisk Tidende revealed that there were 3 United States Senators and 7 Congressmen with Norwegian blood in their veins. They were Senators Warren Magnuson (Washington), Edward J. Thye (Minnesota), and Alexander Wiley (Wisconsin), Congressmen Henry Jackson and Thor C. Tollefson (Washington), August Andresen, Harold C. Hagen, and Harold Knutson (Minnesota), Henry O. Talle (Iowa), and Leroy Johnson (California).

November 2   By 1948, a large percentage of Scandinavian-Americans had returned to the Republican Party, although Harry S. Truman ran very well in the heavily concentrated Scandinavian areas of the nation.

Hubert H. Humphrey, whose mother was born on a farm near Kristiansand, Norway, was elected to the United States Senate from Minnesota.

1950

By 1950 a total of 2,383,486 Scandinavians had come to the United States since their migrations began in 1820. The total for each group was 1,228,113 Swedes, 814,955 Norwegians, and 340,418 Danes.

By 1950, the homogeneous character of the Scandinavians had almost completely disappeared. This was evidenced, for example, by the fact that Scandinavian-Americans could be counted among a variety of religious denominations including the Lutheran, Methodist, Baptist, Catholic, Mormon, and Mission Friends.

AMERICANS ALL----(1950-1970)

By 1970, four generations of Scandinavians have lived on
American soil. What has happened to them, and what is
becoming of them? Time has given us the right to put
the question in the past tense----what did they become?---
for they are no longer Scandinavians; they are Americans.
In the twenty years from 1950 to 1970, very few emigrants
from the Norse countries arrived in the United States.
For example, in 1970, only 722 Swedes, 539 Norwegians
and 602 Danes emigrated to America. For the more than
12,000,000 Americans whose family roots are in Norway,
Sweden and Denmark, the process of assimilation and
Americanization has been almost total. They are spread
throughout the United States, and are active in a variety
of occupations ranging from farmers, artisans and tradespeople, to government clerks, teachers, and small busin-
essmen. They are difficult to pick out as a separate and
distinct ethnic group. Some are brilliant scientists and
scholars, some are politicians and statesmen, and some are
just everyday people who help make this country and this
world go round in this day and age. To set down a long
list of illustrious Scandinavian-Americans, and their ac-
complishments during the last twenty years would be a fut-
ile exercise in name dropping. Instead, the author will
conclude this brief section by simply stating that, on the
whole, it is fair to say that the Scandinavians are a sure-
handed, clear-headed people, sane and sound, and all in
all not unworthy of the opportunities they found in the
United States. No one will deny that the position occupied
by the United States in the world today could never have
been attained but for the periodic inflows of population
over a long span. If for no other reason than the fact that
the masses from Scandinavia acted as farmers, workers
and consumers in a new and rapidly developing country,
Americans owe them a debt of gratitude. The fact that
the Scandinavians did more than that is a tribute not only
to their own talents, but to the creative environment they
found in America.

DOCUMENTS

What is contained in the document section of this volume is but a fraction of the relatively vast amount of available primary material concerned with Scandinavian immigration to and in the United States. Obviously much more could have been included, but space limitations precluded the author from doing so. However, the documents printed on the following pages were selected to give the reader a broad spectrum of the diverse aspects of the Scandinavian movement to America, and to act as a starting point for those students interested in pursuing the subject further.

Three problems exist with reference to documents relative to Scandinavian immigration. First, there is no central repository of primary materials concerned with the movement; second, a large number of the documents have, as yet, not been translated into English; and finally, many have already been published or reprinted in other works, limiting their availability for this volume, due to the copyright statutes. In addition, almost no primary material concerned with Danish immigration is to be found.

Despite these difficulties, materials can be obtained, although they are widely scattered, in a variety of places, across the United States. A few, relative to the subject, are contained in the Bureau of Immigration and Naturalization's Records, but they deal, for the most part, with statistical information. The University of Minnesota has in its collections, a number of primary documents dealing with the topic, as does the Norwegian-American Historical Association at Northfield, Minnesota. Upsala College of East Orange, New Jersey is a repository of the Reports and Yearbooks of the Swedish Augustana Lutheran Church, although many of these materials are still in their original Swedish, and few have been catalogued or indexed.

Finally, I would like to thank the Norwegian-American Historical Association for allowing me to reprint some of the materials included in this documents section.

In the fourteenth century, an expedition under the leadership of Paul Knutson was sent out by the King of Norway and Sweden to search for lost Scandinavian settlers of the Greenland colony.   Finding no trace of them in Greenland, Knutson sailed westward reaching Narragansett Bay in 1355. It is believed he proceeded inland as far as Minnesota's lake region. Many years later, a farmer near Kensington, Minnesota in 1898, dug up a large stone slab with runic symbols.

(Source: Hjalmer R. Holand, Westward From Vinland and America, New York, 1940.)

[We are] 8 Goths [Swedes] and 22 Norwegians on an exploration jour- ney from Vinland round about the West. We had camped by [a lake with] 2 skerries one day's journey north from this stone   We were [out] and fish- ed one day   After we came home [we] found 10 of our men red with blood and dead AV [E] M [ARIA] save [us] from evil. . . year . . . 1362

The selections cited here are part of the extraordinarily well-preserved collection of documents concerned with the New Sweden colony of the early seventeenth century. They include an excerpt from the "Instructions" Governor Johan Printz carried with him from Sweden to America, and three documents relating to Indian-Swedish relations.
(Source: Amandus Johnson, ed., The Instructions For Johann Printz, Philadelphia, 1930, pp. 82-92.)
(Source: Amandus Johnson, The Swedes on the Delaware, Philadelphia, 1915.)

And if the Governor does not find it. . . necessary at once . . . to fortify another new place, but can for the present properly get along with Fort Christina, then he shall so much the more urge and arrange about agriculture and the cultivation of the land, setting and urging the people thereto with zeal and energy, exerting himself, before all other things, that so much seed-corn may be committed to the ground that the tenants may derive therefrom their necessary food. . . .

Next to this, he shall pay good and close attention to the cultivation of tobacco and appoint thereto a certain number of laborers, pressing the matter so that that cultivation may increase. . . so that he can send over a good quantity of tobacco on all ships coming hither. . . .

That it may be better arranged for [the increase of] cattle and all kinds of live stock. . . the Governor shall in the beginning exert himself to obtain a good breed of all kinds of cattle, and above or besides that which is sent out from here, also seek to purchase necessary additions from the neighboring. . . English, distributing all such [cattle] among those who use and take care of fields, in exchange for grain, and in the manner he may find most serviceable to the stockholders. . . .

Among and above other things, he shall direct his attention to sheep, to obtain them of good breed, and gradually seek to establish as many sheepfolds as he possibly can, so that in the future a good and considerable quantity of wool may be shipped over here.

The peltry-trade with the wild [people] he shall also, so far as possible, seek to keep in a good state, exercise and keep inspection over the commissioners appointed for the purpose of trading with the Indians, to prevent all frauds, and take care that [Her] Roy [al] Maj [esty] and her subjects, and the members interested in this Company, may have reason to expect good returns from their cargoes. Likewise he shall see to it that no one. . . may be permitted to traffic with the natives in peltries; but such trace shall alone be carried on by persons thereto appointed in the name of the whole Company and on its behalf.

Whatever else of useful things is, gradually, to be done in that country, time and circumstances there on the spot will best give the Governor advice. Especially as this land, New Sweden, is situated in a climate with Portugal; so. . . it is to be supposed that salt-works might be established on the sea-coast. But in case the salt could not be perfectly evaporated by the . . . sun, yet, at the least, the salt water might thereby so far be improved that it might afterwards be perfectly condensed by means of fire, without great labor and expense; which the Governor must have in mind and try. . . .

And as almost everywhere on the ground wild grapevines and grapes are found, and the climate seems to be favorable to wine culture, therefore the Governor shall also direct his thoughts in that direction, that, as time goes on, such culture, and what further belongs to it, may be established and improved.

He can also have close and careful search made in all places as to whether any metals or minerals are to be found in the country, and, if there are any and can be discovered, send hither all full information about it. . . .

Out of the over-abundant forests, the Governor shall consider and try how and in what manner profit may be made from the good trees of the country; especially what sort of positive advantage may be expected from oak-trees and walnut-trees, since one also could send over here a good quality as ballast. So it might also be tried, whether oil might not advantageously be pressed out of the walnuts.

How and where fisheries might best and with good advantage be established for profit, the Governor shall there likewise take into consideration and let himself be correctly informed; especially as it is reported that in. . . Godin's Bay, and thereabouts, at a certain season of the year, whale fishery can be advantageously prosecuted and arranged. Therefore, he shall have an eye upon this and send over hither all needed information . . .

The Governor shall also diligently proceed, and inform himself, if [there are] good sustenance and convenience for keeping in that country a large quantity of silkworms, wherewith some manufacture might be carried on. And if he perceives and finds that something useful might therewith be accomplished, he shall have in mind that for such purpose every proper arrangement might gradually be made.

INDIAN RELATIONS

Indian Deed of Land.

A. D. 1654, on July 8, the Sachems Peminacka and Ahopameck came to Fort Christina, where they began to talk about their lands, which belong to them. Thus Peminacka, the sachem, presented to the Swedes all the right and pretention which he, as rightful owner, had to these lands, namely: Tamakonck or the Sandhock with the surrounding lands, so also all the land all the way from Fort Christina up the river which has not yet been bought, especially Naamans Point to Marikens point inclusive with all its pretentions. Ahopameck, as the rightful owner, also presented to the Swedes all the land, which is located, all the way from Marikis Hook, all the way to half of the Skulkijll, Tennakonck and other [lands] unmentioned, which has been sold of other rightful owners, together with Kinsassingh, Arunameck, Mockorhuttingh, Kokarakungh, with all the lands and waters, which are subject to it, Passaijungh excepted. [They] testify and declare that these lands have been their own and are not bought by any one in particular before. Wherefore they and their descendants herewith sell all these aforesaid lands . . . For further surety they confirmed this with their marks and witnesses who were present, placing their signatures below. Made at Christina as above.

Peminacka as the rightful owner
Ahopameck as the rightful owner.

Johan Risingh   Gregorius van Dijck

Testimony of the Heirs of Mitatsimint.

We the undersigned heirs of the deceased Sachem Mitatsimint give by this our writing the testimony that the land lying below Appachaihackingh unto Mettocksinowousingh, belongs to no one else than to us, Peminacka being allowed to hunt upon Quinamkot but not as the owner to sell the same. We also know that the late Sachem Mitatsimint bargained about the said land with the Swedes, wherefore, for a confirmation, we have desired, as the true heirs and owners, by this our drawn up contract to testify that no one else, be [it] what nation it may, has a right or pretention to dwell upon the aforesaid lands or to incorporate [them] than the Swedes alone, for which [lands] we also have been contended by them, like our deceased sachem and father. Besides [we] will show (prove) by the savages in the entire river that the aforesaid land has been the property not of Pemenacka but of Mitatsimint, and [this] we as his heirs herewith maintain for a testimony of the truth, subscribing [to it] with the marks of our own hands.

. . . . Wherefore Peminacka desired to confirm herewith the said purchase, which the Swedes had closed with him, as the rightful owner of the said land, which Metatsimint had presented to him before the purchase and before his death, so that none hereafter may find cause to object to or censure this. This they certify with their marks. Done at Fort Christina, the day and date given above.

Peminacka, as rightful owner, Ahopameck, as witness, Sinques(?) AS WITNESS, Pinnar (?) [as w] itness. Johan Risingh, Jan Ja[nss] on Bockhorn, Gregorius [va]n Dijck, Johan (?) [Papegoja?]

Dated, Elsborgh, July 3, 1651
The mark of Kiapes the son of Mitatsimint.
The mark of Notike the widow of Mitatsimint.
The mark of the two children of Mitatsimint.

As witnesses:
Peter Johimson.
Gothefryd Harmer.

See how good are these friends who have given us these gifts. We shall be as one body and one soul. If in the time of Governor Printz, the Big Belly, we were friendly, we shall now be as a calabash [pipe or bowl] without a crack or crevice and with you we want to make a pact of everlasting friendship. If some one attacks you, even in the middle of the night, we shall come to your aid, and if some one attacks us, though it is in the middle of the night, you must come to our aid.

In 1683, William Penn wrote a memorable paragraph, which appears in his The Present State of His Majesty's Isles and Territories in America, concerned with the character and nature of the Swedish colonists who had been incorporated into his own colony of Pennsylvania.
(Source: William Penn, The Present State of His Majesty's Isles and Territories in America, London, 1687.)

The first planters in these parts were the Dutch, and soon after them the Swedes and the Finns. The Dutch applied themselves to traffic, the Swedes and the Finns to husbandry. The Dutch have a meeting place for religious worship in New Castle [Fort Casimir] and the Swedes one at Christina [Wilmington], one at Tinicum, and one at Wicaco, within half a mile of this town [Philadelphia]. The Swedes inhabit the freshes of the River Delaware. There is no need of giving any description of them, who are better known in England than here; but they are plain, strong, industrious people, yet have made no great progress in the culture or propagation of fruit trees, as if they desired rather to have enough than plenty or traffic. But I presume the Indians made them the more careless, by furnishing them with the means of profit, to wit, skins and furs for rum, and such strong liquors. They kindly received me, as well as the English, who were few before the people concerned with me came among them. I must needs to commend their respect to authority, and kind behavior to the English. They do not degenerate from the old friendship between both kingdoms. As they are people proper and strong of body, so they have fine children, and almost every house full; rare to find one of them without three or four boys, and as many girls: some six, seven, and eight sons. And I must do them that right, I see few young men more sober and laborious."

In 1758, the Reverend Israel Acrelius, one of the last Swedish Lutheran ministers in America, wrote bitterly about the waning of Swedish culture and language in the areas that had once belonged to New Sweden. These excerpts accurately foreshadowed the almost total English assimilation of the remaining Swedes.

(Source: Amandus Johnson, The Swedes on the Delaware, Philadelphia, 1915.)

Formerly, the church people could come some Swedish miles on foot to church; now the young, as well as the old, must be upon horseback. Then many a good and honest man rode upon a piece of bear-skin; now scarcely any saddle is valued unless it has a saddle-cloth with galloon and fringe. Then servants and girls were seen in church barefooted; now young people will be like persons of quality in their dress . . . .

Sometimes it is concluded in the Vestry that no more English preaching shall be held, no English any more be buried in the grave-yard. Then the Minister and his Church officers are decried as persons who regard all English as heathens . . . So this must be changed again.

One will have his child baptized in English, another in Swedish, at one and the same hour in the Church. Some refuse to stand as Sponsors if the child is not baptized in Swedish, and yet it may be that the other Sponsors do not understand it . . . When funeral sermons are preached, English people of every form of faith come together, and then it often happens that the one desires preaching in English, the other in Swedish, and that just as the Minister is going into the Church.

It is here necessary to state how far these Swedish churches are inclined to have their service in English. The Swedes formerly dwelt more closely together, used their language more among themselves and daily at home in their houses; when it happens that the old among our people do not speak English well, can hardly read an English book or clearly understand English preaching; and, in a word they hate in their hearts everything that is English. They say that they are Swedish people, although they are in an English country.

Some of the young people have learnt both languages, and bring up their children in the same manner, as they speak Swedish in their houses, and let the children take their chance of learning English outside the house . . . All those who understand and speak and read Swedish are entirely in favor of Divine service in their own language. Others, again, whose wives, children, relatives and friends are English, cannot but desire worship for them in that language which they understand, especially as they, upon their side, contribute to support the Minister and church, are descendants of Swedes, and do not wish to fall away from their church, and have also many members of the English church among them, who in like manner need Divine Service, and will help to support the Minister.

Cleng Peerson, often called the "Pathfinder" of Norwegian emigration, first came to the United States in 1824, as an advance agent of a group of emigrants. He wrote to his father, what many consider to be, the first "America Letter" describing his journey and the new country he had explored.

(Source: Theodore C. Blegen, "Cleng Peerson and Norwegian Immigration," Mississippi Valley Historical Review, March, 1921.)

Blegen gave the full details of this letter and the mystery surrounding its authenticity in, Theodore C. Blegen, Norwegian Migration to America, 1825-1860, Northfield, Minnesota, 1931.)

New York, December 20, 1824

Dear Father, Brother, Sister, Brother-in-Law, and Friends:---

I let you know that I have arrived in America happy and well. After a journey of six weeks we reached New York, where I found all my friends in good health and they received me very affectionately. We remained there five days; then we took the steamboat "William Penn" for Albany, which is 150 miles, that is 30 Norwegian miles, it cost two dollars for each of us and we also received free board, where we arrived in 24 hours. Later we went to Troy, and then westward through the great canal 200 miles to Salina Salt Works, paying our way by working; thereafter we took another boat and went the rest of the way to my friends in Faningtown [Farmington] , where I left my comrade. I then went overland to Geneva, where the land commissioner lives, to buy land for myself and for you, as previously discussed. The land commissioner is very friendly, and has promised to give us as much aid as possible. We reached an agreement in regard to six pieces of land which I have selected, and shall be held for us until next fall. I already have a house in process of building, 12 ells long and 10 ells wide, which I hope to complete by New Year's day. We then expect winter for a couple of months which will be a good time to haul wood from the forests. When I was in Rochester I bought a stove for 20 dollars with full equipment such as pans, pots for meat, a baking oven, and other things; so we shall not need any fireplace. I have built this house on the land selected for you whose arrival I am waiting, but in the spring, if the Lord permits me to live, I shall build on my own land. I have 5 acres of land, which is 330 per arec [i], to have ready in the spring to sow and plant. I have a cow in Faningtun [Farmington] which cost me ten dollars, and a few sheep. I have reported the prices of all things in Knud Eie's letter. I am very much concerned in my mind about your coming to America. When I think of my sister and of other friends of mine, oh, how I wish that that time were over, and how glad I would be to receive word that you were coming to New York that I might greet you there. I have no doubt that you will be able to journey through the canal very comfortably and at a cheap rate. The Friends in Masedon [Macedon] have promised and said that my sister and the others shall stay with them until we get houses built for them. Well, many persons are buying land in this vicinity; there are many cultivated pieces of land here that we may work on share. It will soon be filled up around here and especially nearest the canal. I must leave everything to Providence; what He wills, you also do. You must not let yourselves be frightened away by talk. I have found the help of Providence as long as I have kept steadfast in hope; that is all we can do...

On October 9, 1825, fourteen weeks after she had left Stavanger, Norway, the sloop <u>Restaurationen</u> sailed into New York Harbor, bringing the first large group of Norwegian emigrants to the United States. Two local newspapers commented upon her arrival under the caption, "A Novel Sight." (Source: New York Evening Post, October 10, 1825; <u>New York Daily Advertiser</u>, October 15, 1825.)

Arrived last evening (October 9, 1825). Danish Sloop <u>Restauration</u>, Holland, 98 days from Norway, via Long Island Sound, with iron to Boorman and Johnson, 52 passengers . . . .

The vessel is very small, measuring, as we understand, only about 360 Norwegian lasts, or 45 American tons, and brought 52 passengers, male and female, all bound for Ontario County, where an agent who came over sometime since, purchased a tract of land.

The appearance of such a party of strangers, coming from so distant a country and in a vessel of a size apparently ill calculated for a voyage across the Atlantic could not but excite an unusual degree of interest. An enterprise like this argues a good deal of boldness in the master of the vessel as well as an adventurous spirit in the passengers . . . . Those who came from the farms are dressed in coarse cloths of domestic manufacture, of a fashion different from the American, but those who inhabit the town wear calicos, ginghams and gay shawls, imported, we presume, from England. The vessel is built on the model common to fishing boats on that coast, with a single mast and topsail, sloop-rigged.

In this selection, a Norwegian immigrant describes pioneering in Illinois, and thinks of moving on. These passages come from Johannes Nordboe's letter to Hans Larsen Rudi, dated April 30, 1837.
(Source: Arne Odd Johnson, ed., "Johannes Nordboe and Norwegian Immigration, An American Letter of 1837," VIII, Norwegian-American Studies and Records, Northfield, Minnesota, 1934.)

WE intend to move [to western Missouri] in a few weeks. We must first sell eighty acres of land we have here, and we will auction off a ten-acre field of wheat, together with our livestock, which includes 7 oxen, 4 cows, and 1 mare. Last summer we were so unfortunate as to lose, by accident, a large and expensive driving ox ($36), a hog, and 4 calves. The 7 oxen, 4 cows, 1 mare, 4 swine, and 20 hens, together with the eighty acres, all of which must be converted into money, should net us $200 and the wheat field $100. With as much as $300 to begin with when we come to the state of Missouri, we hope with God's help to do well.

This western country is far different from the eastern states. Perhaps you will recall what I said the last time I talked with you---that I would not stop in my travels until I had reached the westernmost part of Missouri. I believe God revealed this to me long before I left Norway .... N.B. It is very easy to raise cattle here and also to till the soil. This year as well as last we have had nothing with which to feed the cattle except what my two sons have cut on the prairie, amounting to about thirty tons (a ton is two thousand pounds). We have had no stable for the cattle this winter, since stables are not used here, which is unfortunate. The winter is very cold, and this second winter has again been long.

The land in the state of Illinois is largely prairie, with little woodland except along the rivers and creeks. The summers are extremely beautiful. Then the whole country, both woodland and prairie, is bedecked with grass and flowers of all colors, which bloom from the earliest spring to late autumn. When some fall, others come up. Some big, yellow ones in the autumn have stalks ten feet high. The summer may be compared to an earthly paradise, but the winter, on the contrary may be likened to a mountain climate.

Here the fields are prepared in the following way: The sod, two and a half inches thick, is turned over by a large plow that cuts strips sixteen, eighteen, twenty, and in some cases twenty-four inches wide. The plow is drawn by five and sometimes six pair of oxen, but most frequently by five. The land broken in the spring is ready by August to be harrowed and sowed with wheat for the next summer, but usually it is allowed to lie until the following spring. It is then plowed with one or two pair of oxen; and corn, wheat, oats, or whatever one pleases is planted. The field is then in fine condition without any need of fertilizer ....

Of Indian corn or maize there are also many varieties. There is much to write about, but space will not permit. Deer are plentiful. They are mostly hunted by Indians, for others do not have time for such things. My son Peder is now away chopping cordwood. As he is not yet full-grown, he cannot earn more than a dollar a day. Wages for labor are very high here. A full-grown man can earn from $150 to $160 in wages in one year. Here a poor man can soon become a well-to-do farmer if he works hard and uses good sense. He can look forward to becoming rich without usury, a difficult task in Norway . . . . . .

The woods are largely oaks, three varieties of walnut, and small hazel bushes. They all bear large quantities of nuts that are good for human beings and of great benefit to swine. These may be sold in town for a dollar a bushel . . . .

N.B. When we arrived in New York, I was old and poor, with small children. I could not earn much, for they did not wish to employ old people for work. If I had had $20 for a deposit, I could have bought land at $5 to $6 per acre, with interest at 7 per cent. Other Norwegians who secured land made a profit from their labor of $200, others $300 to $400, and so on. Some made $1,500 to $1,600, depending on how poor they had been, and one who has not yet arrived here, had only $3 when he came, newly married, healthy, and strong, in 1825. When he sells his improved farm, he will have $2,000. Others who came here bought land and are already well established. Those who had already come from Ohio and other states are now wealthy.

It was because of me that the Norwegians came here. I have always been of service to others, but never to myself. When we came here, the land had been surveyed for some time but was not settled, except by a few who are now rich. Then it became known that the land was to be sold at auction. The other Norwegians each bought a piece of land they had claimed at the Congress price of ten shillings---$1.25--per acre. It is the low price that has enriched so many. I had to go forty miles northward where there were no human beings except a few Indians.

Even though it was in the wilderness, the piece of land I selected was the best and most desirable I have ever seen. During the winter I returned to the place. With the help of my son and son-in-law, I cut and hauled timber for a house, but since we could not begin to live in it until late in the spring and I became ill in the fall and continued ill through the winter, we had to sell our rights to the large and beautiful farm for $400. This happened last year, and not until then had we begun to get ahead a little . . . . . .

If I am lucky enough to find good, satisfactory land where we are now going, I shall take four claims, each of 160 acres, which is a farm large enough for one family. N.B. One for me, one for each of my three sons, perhaps, one for my brother, if possible . . . . Our daughter will remain here. They have done well, have 130 acres, have worked on it for two and a half years, and paid $150 for the farm. If he sold his farm now, he could get $1,400 to $1,500. They have 2 pair of oxen, 3 cows, 6 sheep, many swine, 4 geese, and a great many chickens. Last year a son was born to them, a sound and healthy one.

I am afraid that this is scarcely readable, for I see so poorly and have no suitable spectacles. I hope you will excuse me. I am now 69 years old, my wife 36, my daughter 22, my eldest son 17, the second 15, and third 12 years of age.

Ole Rynning was 28 when he undertook to lead a group of Norwegians to America. Sailing with 84 emigrants, he arrived in the United States in 1837. During the following year, he wrote a 39 page pamphlet, which was so widely read that the increase in Norwegian immigration in the 1840's is attributed to its influence.
(Source: Ole Rynning, A True Account of America for the Information and Help of Peasant and Commoner, Christiania, 1838, translated by Theodore C. Blegen as Ole Rynning's True Account of America, Minnesota, 1917.)

. . . The most important country in all America with respect to population as well as to freedom and happy form of government is the "United States" in North America. Usually, therefore, this country is meant when you hear someone speak of America in an indefinite way. It is to this land your countrymen have emigrated; it is this land which I shall now describe.

. . . . The immigrants of different nations are not equally well received by the Americans. From Ireland there comes yearly a great rabble, who, because of their tendency to drunkenness, their fighting and their knavery, make themselves commonly hated. A respectable Irishman hardly dares acknowledge his nationality. The Norwegians generally have thus far a good reputation for their industry, trustworthiness and readiness with which the more well to do have helped poor people through the country . . . .

For the comfort of the faint-hearted, I can, therefore, declare with truth that in America, as in Norway, there are laws, government and authorities. But everything is designed to maintain the natural freedom and equality of men. In regard to the former, everyone is free to engage in whatever honorable occupation he wishes, and go wherever he wishes . . . . Only the real criminal is threatened with punishment by the law.

. . . . An ugly contrast to this freedom and equality which justly constitute the pride of the Americans is the infamous slave traffic, which is tolerated and still flourishes in the southern states. In these states is found a race of black people, with wooly hair on their heads, who are called negroes, and who are brought here from Africa, which is their native country; these poor beings are bought and sold just as other property, and are driven to work with a whip or scourge like horses or oxen. If a master whips his slave to death or shoots him dead in a rage, he is not looked upon as a murderer. The children born of a negress are slaves from birth, even if their father is a white man. . . .

Two schools have now been started among the Norwegians at Fox River, where the children learn English; but the Norwegian language seems to be destined to die out with the parents. At least, the children do not learn to read Norwegian. At Beaver Creek no school is yet established, but most of the children who are old enough are taken into American homes, where their instruction is usually well cared for . . . .

AMERICAN FEVER--1839-1840

The publication of Ole Rynning's "America Book" had an immediate affect upon emigration from Norway to the United States. The following three selections are excerpts describing the growth of "American Fever" in two areas of Norway, Numedal and Snaasen.
(Source: Billed-Magazin, I, 94; Billed-Magazin, I, 154; Billed-Magazin, I, 45.)

I remained in Numedal throughout the winter and until the following spring. The report of my return spread like wildfire through the land, and an incredible number of people came to America. Many traveled as far as twenty Norwegian miles to talk with me. It was impossible to answer all the letters which came to me containing questions in regard to conditions on the other side of the ocean. In the spring of 1839 about one hundred persons from Numedal stood ready to go with me across the sea. Amongst these were many farmers and heads of families, all, except the children, able-bodied and persons in their best years. In addition to these were some from Telemarken and from Numedal who were unable to go with me as our ship was full . . . .

Hardly any other Norwegian publication has been purchased and read with such avidity as this Rynning's Account of America. People traveled long distances to hear "news" from the land of wonders, and many who before were scarcely able to read began in earnest to practice in the "America-book" making such progress that they were soon able to spell their way forward and acquire most of the contents. The sensation created by Ansten's return was much the same as that which one might imagine a dead man would create, were he to return to tell of the life beyond the grave. Throughout the winter he was continually surrounded by groups who listened attentively to his stories. Since many came long distances in order to talk with him, the reports of the far west were soon spread over a large part of the country. Ministers and bailiffs . . . . tried to frighten us with terrible tales about the dreadful sea monsters, and about man-eating wild animals in the new world; but when Ansten Nattestad had said "Yes and Amen" to Rynning's Account, all fears and doubts were removed . . . .

For a time I believed that half of the population of Snaasen had lost their senses. Nothing else was spoken of but the land that flows with milk and honey. Our minister, Ole Rynning's father, tried to stop the fever. Even from the pulpit he urged people to be discreet and described the hardships of the voyage and the cruelty of the American savage in the most forbidding colors. This was only pouring oil upon the fire . . . . Ole Rynning was one of those philanthropists for whom no sacrifice is too great if it can only contribute to the happiness of others. He was, in the fullest sense, a friend of the people, the spokesman of the poor and one whose mouth never knew deceit . . . . But then came the news; Ole Rynning is no more. This acted as cold water upon the blood of the people. The report of his death caused sorrow throughout the whole parish, for few have been so commonly loved as this man. Now the desire to emigrate cooled also, and many of those who formerly had spoken most enthusiastically in favor of emigration now shuddered with fear at the thought of America's unhealthful climate . . . .

As Norwegian emigrants prepared to leave the Old Country, and come to America, scores of songs and poems were written by the emigrants themselves, telling of their reasons for leaving Norway, and what they expected to find in the New World.   The following selections are a few excerpts of the many poems and songs that have survived.

(Source: Morgenbladet, February 27, 1846, translation by Martin Ruud; Nordlyset (Muskego, Wisconsin), August 19, 1847, reprinted in Hjalmar Holand, De Norske Settlementers Historie, 57-58, translated by Martin Ruud in Studies and Records of the Norwegian-American Association, II, 4-5, - 1927; "Farvel til Pastor G.F. Dietrichson, i Anledning hans Afreise til Amerika," in Stavanger Amstidende og Adresseavis, April 26, 1851; Blegen, Northfield, Minnesota, 1931.) Nils J. Qvarme, "Arbeiderforenings Sang," in Arbeider-Foreningernes Blad, July 20, 1850; Blegen, Norwegian Migration to America, Northfield, Minnesota, 1931.) Christian Olsen, Kvoeldstunder, Nytaarsgave, 1862. Nogle Digte af Rungolf, 81-85, Christiania, 1862; originally published in Morgenbladet, April 30, 1861, reprinted in Decorah-Posten, (Decorah, Iowa), March 27, 1925, translated by Martin Ruud in Studies and Records of the Norwegian-American Historical Association, II, 16-18; Christian Monsen, Samlede Digte, Trondhjem, 1854, 346-49.

I am not going to stay in Norway any longer.   I am going to America; that's the best thing for me to do.   I have heard that men who know how to use their hands can live well there.   Land is cheap, and heavy taxes don't eat up everything a farmer makes.

You hear in this country a lot of fine talk about liberty and equality and that the people hold the purse-strings; but the bureaucrats are paid too well, while the common people must struggle along.   The government brags about undertakings that must cost a barrel of gold; at the same time economic life is strangled by all sorts of restrictions and crushed by tariffs.

Poor peasant lads are drafted for military service, while the rich man's sons escape.   That's Norwegian equality.   Have they forgotten the provision of the constitution: The defense of the kingdom is a duty resting upon all.   Shall we never remedy such abuses?   Will people stand such things forever?

Farewell, Norway, and God bless thee.   Stern and severe wert thou always, but as a mother I honor thee, even though thou skimped my bread. All things vanish.   Grief and care sink down upon the heart; still the memory of thee refreshes the soul like the deep sleep of a child.

Other lands offer me independence, and for my labor well-being to my children.   These, O Norway, thou didst not give me, for thou art a land of lords and slaves, where the great ones ruled and we obeyed.

Once more, God bless thee; to the day of my death I will pray God to keep thee; for thou wert the keeper of my childhood and the joys of childhood thou gavest me.   I will remember thee always, whatever life may bring, and I will pray, "Throw off the chains that embittered my youth for me."

Far away, beyond the dark sea waves, is blossoming forth that great land of liberty. There, deep in age-old forests, on green fields, or beside silver-blue waters, many a little Norway is now springing-up. For Norwegian brothers ---ah, by the thousands -- have been fated by the Norns to leave their loved mountains, to depart from ancestral lands in peaceful valleys.

And now the great throng, whose departure we have witnessed, who have crossed the sea to the distant strand, look back, with longing and with emotion, to the mother church in the land of their youth. For it gathered them in its tender arms; it cradled Norway's sons while they grew strong and great; in that church they dreamed the brightest dreams of their lives and learned the Heavenly precepts of truth and peace.

Over there our brothers sat in the shadow of death; unheard was the pure word of life; but now temples are built there for the worship of God and under their arches abides the Holy Spirit. And we are sending over a pious band of apostles, who, guided by heavenly angels, shall light for our brothers divine beacons pointing the way to our better home.

They go aboard; the old man stands motionless on the shore gazing at the ship, like Mother Norway herself lamenting the going of her children.

The winds swell the flapping sails, and the ship glides majestically out to sea. The groves fade away, and the deep valley and the mountain peaks are lost in the mists.

Farewell---the last word of parting. The storms from the North shall shout it, and the little billows gliding softly off-shore shall sing it like a threnody heard in dreams.

And yet, even now, when the last skerry has disappeared, the brothers still stand gazing fixedly at the spot where the last glimpse of the fatherland vanished away.

To the west, where the dazzling sun sinks down to hide behind dark blue waves, a golden cloud drifts away until, hanging over California forests, it catches a reflection that we can glimpse of the riches Heaven gave the western world.

Away, away then, with courage high! For fortune awaits the brave. Even as our bark turns its prow stoutly against the angry, foaming billows, so, with light hearts, we face the dangers that await us, with hope in our souls and trust in God.

To thee, beloved land, I bid farewell. Soon I no longer shall view thy beauty nor hear the music of thy waterfalls. Thy snow-capped mountains will fade from sight and slowly thy coast will sink away in the mists like a mother being lowered in the grave. No glimpse then of thy tallest peaks; only a lonely sail on the boundless deep.

This selection is part of a letter written by Gustav Unonius, the founder of New Uppsala colony in Wisconsin. In it, he describes the origins of his new settlement, and the conditions that new Scandinavian immigrants will find in America. The first part of the document is a note from the editor of Aftonbladet, the Swedish newspaper in which the Unonius letter first appeared.
(Source: Augustana Historical Society Publications, VII, Rock Island, Illinois, 1937.)

[Aftonbladet, January 4, 5, 1842]

The editor has had the pleasure of receiving for publication the following most interesting communication from Mr. G. Unonius, a young clerk, who is not entirely unknown as the publisher of a group of poems and who last summer with his wife and a couple of other Swedes emigrated to the United States of North America. Mr. Unonius wishes to make known that he uses this method of informing, all at one time, his friends and acquaintances who are interested in his fate, especially those around Upsala, but his communication will surely be read with marked pleasure by each and every one.

Milwaukee, October 13, 1841.

After our arrival at New York the 10th of September last, we left there the 17th and went on board the steamboat "Rochester" for Albany, from whence the journey was further continued by canal boat on the Erie Canal to Buffalo, where it became necessary for us to stop for a few days, after which, on an exceptionally fine steamboat, the "Illinois," we entered upon the journey over the great inland lakes, around the Michigan peninsula to Milwaukee, a little five-year-old city with 3500 inhabitants, located eighty miles north of Chicago on Lake Michigan. It is the capital of Milwaukee County, Wisconsin Territory. We have lived there for two weeks, during which time I have had occasion to journey on foot into the interior and in the midst of these wonderfully beautiful valleys to select our future home. Yesterday we began cutting the timber for our little log house, and in two weeks we hope to be able to move in. In the meantime we shall lodge in a hut built of the boards that later will form the floor and the roof of our cottage. As yet, however, we have not left the city . . . .

I have now been in America over a month; during this time I have traveled about 1800 English miles into the interior, to the Western States, and thus, through conversation with several persons, I have had the opportunity to learn at least something about the situation and conditions out here. My experience, to be sure, is not great but nevertheless it may perhaps yield several bits of information about one thing or another in the sphere to which it is largely confined. My intention, which is about to be realized, was to settle in the New World as a colonist or farmer. Before my departure from the fatherland I found many who shared my view and in the future perhaps intended to carry it out. I am fulfilling a promise by imparting the slight information I am now able to give, which for the emigrant to western America, perhaps, is not so insignificant. I do not want to write anything except what I know, and this probably would be impressive enough if it were not that the size of the letter, the time, and the expensive postage together compel me to be brief. America is judged and described so differently---few know it properly; in my opinion, at least a ten years' residence, continuous traveling, and association with all classes of people are necessary. The people here are everything. One can travel through the country and describe it in a short time, but the people, the character of the nation, should be studied, and for this several years are insufficient. Just think of the composition of the American population. Is it not a mixture of families from all parts of Europe? How can a hurried trip give a fair impression of the whole, in its parts so different? I am sure I shall never be able to do it completely. Yet many with as little knowledge of America as I possess have written, described, and philosophized. This accounts for the many untruths that are spread around in Europe about America, some to its advantage and others, perhaps the most, to its disadvantage. A traveler visits Boston, Philadelphia, etc., and thinks he is competent to pass judgement on the United States. As though a visitor to Paris could absorb all that is necessary to describe Europe! A person spends a short time in New York and afterward talks and writes about America! That is like judging all of Sweden on the basis of Stockholm. Read Tocqueville's Democracy in America. In my opinion, he has given the most accurate portrayal of conditions. I believe I am already able to contradict several of Miss Trollope's statements; and in regard to the interesting travelogues of our Swedes, Arfwedson and Gosselman, they have perhaps also, in consequence of the more fortunate circumstances in which they lived and the circles to which they had access, been guilty of the mistake of having presented all in a glittering form. I was told by a Swede in New York that a foreigner with capital ought not to settle in America because he would become impoverished in a short time. Perhaps he was right; I do not know and I shall never be able to verify it by experience. But what I do know is that a man without capital, through thrift and foresight, can advance and perhaps produce capital. Yet he has many obstacles to overcome and great difficulties to endure. . . . I came here with very little money, and in the beginning the emigrant meets with considerable expense. At all events far be it from me to influence others and to persuade compatriots at home to abandon the fatherland and to take up their abode in a strange part of the world. People in Sweden who have an assured living ought not to exchange a pleasant home for unknown dangers and an unknown fate. Even those in the homeland who, like myself, are doomed to a future of indebtedness and dependency, either thronging the civil service or bowing in the antechambers or as farmers burdened with taxes and not owning their plots of land or as narrowly-defined craft workers lacking opportunity to work---all should carefully examine and deliberate before they bid farewell to a country which, no matter what our fate may be, will always be remembered with regret and love, if for no other reason than the tender bonds of relationship and friendship which unites us with the fatherland. Duty and promise prompt me to request that an extract from this letter to those friends at home may be inserted in one of the newspapers of Sweden.

A young Swedish immigrant-pioneer, John Friman, in a letter sent home to Sweden, reflected on his first meeting with Gustav Unonius, and his new home at New Uppsala, Wisconsin.
(Source: Skara Tidning, May 18, 1843, in Augustana Historical Society Publications, VII, Rock Island, Illinois, 1937.)

We are healthier and more vigorous than we ever were in Sweden. Many people from England and Ireland have already come here. Last fall, in October, a few Swedes from Upsala came here from Milwaukee, Mr. Gustaf Unonius and wife, married only six weeks when they left Sweden. A relative, Inspector Groth, and a Doctor Palman have settled on a beautiful lake near a projected canal, twenty-eight miles west of Milwaukee, Milwaukee County. They have named the settlement New Upsala and the capital of New Sweden in Wisconsin. They are expecting several families and students from Upsala this summer.

. . . I visited New Upsala last fall. They wanted me to sell out and move there. Father has probably heard of them. Last fall Unonius wrote to Aftonbladet. I hope his letter will awaken the desire to emigrate among the Swedes . . . . Altogether we own two hundred acres of land, and when we have our farm fenced and eighty acres broken. . . . I wouldn't trade it for a whole estate in Sweden, with all its ceremonies. Out here in the woods we know nothing of such . . . . Give our love to Herman and say to him that we hope his health will be better than it was the first time he was here.

In 1844, J. R. Reiersen, one of the early Norwegian settlers in Texas, published a comprehensive Norwegian handbook about America, and especially Texas. He pointed out both the good and bad aspects of life in the United States. This selection is an extract of some of the views he offered prospective Norwegian immigrants.
(Source: J. R. Reiersen, Pathfinder For Norwegian Emigrants to the United North American States and Texas, Norway, 1844.) Translated by Theodore C. Blegen in Studies and Records of the Norwegian-American Historical Association, I, 1926, 110-125.)

All those who have been in America for a few years, with a few individual exceptions are in a contented and independent position. Anxiety and care with respect to daily bread and subsistence for their families burden them no longer. Their cultivated fields yield them a sufficiency of bread stuffs, their cows give them milk and butter in abundance, and their swine furnish them fully with meat. They do not suffer want. Taxes and rent encumber no one, and fear of distraints and seizures does not trouble their minds. Poor rates and begging are practically unknown, and even the children of deceased poor people are eagerly received by the Americans, who support them and give them instruction. But, all things considered, this is as much as one can say . . . .

The majority still live in their original log cabins, which, however, are always a good deal better than the mountain huts in which they lived in Norway. They have only a little money because of the indolence with which many carry on their farming; and the old manner of conducting their household affairs, to which they were accustomed in the old country, is continued. Insanitary conditions obtain in many cases. Lack of efficiency and enterprise---qualities upon which success in America altogether depends---and in general of information and education is among the primary causes which explain why our countrymen have not yet progressed further than they have.

. . . . Immigrants from Voss, Telemarken, Numedal, and elsewhere, have settled in this region and have begun to till the land, but the crops are not yet sufficient to supply the needs of all the settlers. No signs of malaria appeared in the settlement during the first year, but in the following two years, when large numbers of poor immigrants swarmed into the colony---chiefly because it was the nearest Norwegian settlement to Milwaukee---and were lodged, many of them sick as a result of the ocean journey, in the small pioneer huts, a general wave of sickness swept the colony, attacking almost everyone and laying a great many in the grave . . .

Peter Cassel, who had come to Iowa from Sweden in 1845, wrote the following letter on February 9, 1846. In it, he describes the wonders of America in terms that vie with descriptions that came from the pen of Marco Polo during the Middle Ages.
(Source: Östgotha Correspondenten, May 16, 1846.)

The ease of making a living here and the increasing prosperity of the farmers . . . exceeds anything we anticipated. If only half of the work expended on the soil in the fatherland were utilized here, the yield would reach the wildest imagination . . . . Barns and cattle sheds are seldom, if ever, seen in this vicinity; livestock is allowed to roam the year around, and since pasturage is common property, extending from one end of the land to the other, a person can own as much livestock as he desires or can take care of, without the least trouble or expense. . . . One of our neighbors . . . has one hundred head of hogs . . . . Their food consists largely of acorns, a product that is so abundant that as late as February the ground is covered in places . . . Corn fields are more like woods than grain fields . . . .

Freedom and equality are the fundamental principles of the constitution of the United States. There is no such thing as class distinction here, no counts, barons, lords or lordly estates . . . . Everyone lives in the unrestricted enjoyment of personal liberty. A Swedish bonde, raised under oppression and accustomed to poverty and want, here finds himself elevated to a new world, as it were, where all his former hazy ideas of a society conforming more closely to nature's laws are suddenly made real and he enjoys a satisfaction in life that he has never before experienced. There are no beggars here and there never can be so long as the people are ruled by the spirit that prevails now. I have yet to see a lock on a door in this neighborhood . . . . I have never heard of theft . . . . At this time of the year the sap of the sugar maple is running and we have made much sugar and syrup . . . .

CORRESPONDENT FROM THE HOMELAND---1847

In 1847, the Norwegian government sent a prominent lawyer and jurist, Ole Munch Raeder, to the United States to study the operations of the American jury system. Raeder agreed to send home regular dispatches, for newspaper publication, concerned with Norwegian life in America. His descriptions of Norwegian immigrant conditions are probably the most accurate contemporary picture of Norwegian immigrant life in the United States in the 1840's.
(Source: Ole Munch Raeder, America in the Forties, New York, 1929.)

. . . . The trip on the Erie Canal, from Albany to Buffalo, costs only $7.50, including meals, and lasts a day longer than the journey by rail. This price, however, is only for ordinary travelers. The spirit of speculation has led to a rather material reduction in the price for immigrants. Some canal boats, I believe, transport them and their belongings for $2.00, but they have to provide their own food.

The railroads, too, in their case have made an exception to the general rule of having only one class. Sometimes a large boxcar labeled in huge letters "IMMIGRANT CAR", is added to the train, and here the immigrants are piled together in grand confusion, with all their trunks and other belongings. In New York there are companies which arrange the entire journey for immigrants, making their profits through the large masses they transport, as well as whatever they can make through cheating---by dropping them off half way, and so on.

The consul general at New York has made a splendid arrangement for the immigrants whereby they deposit a sum of $6.00 and are then transported to Wisconsin by one of the most dependable companies, which is paid by the consulate upon notification from the immigrant that the company has faithfully discharged its obligation. This plan is announced to the immigrants upon their arrival in New York, but they are so suspicious---or perhaps so unsuspecting when it comes to the Yankees and their agents---that they seldom make use of this splendid means of securing a journey that is both safe and cheap. They cannot resist the temptation of an offer to transport them for a few cents less. The immigrant companies have in their service Norwegians and Swedes who carry on a very profitable business.

On the Great Lakes there is only one means of travel, for immigrants as well as for others, and that is the steamship. The elegance of such a ship is quite remarkable. The vessel is equipped in every possible way for the convenience of the passengers; there is, for example, a barber shop. There is also a band. Its performance on brass instruments we found none too good, but in the evenings it won general approval by presenting comical Negro songs, accompanied by the guitar, and by playing dance music, to which the youthful Yankees executed their favorite cotillion, a sort of quadrille, with many dainty skips and steps. There was also a good piano on board, on which those passengers who thought they knew anything about music frequently tried their skill, more to the horror and dismay than to the enjoyment of their fellow passengers. It was strange to see how easy it was to induce these American ladies, noted in Europe for their prudery and finicality, to play or sing for this audience of absolute strangers from every corner of the earth. . . .

In 1838 the population of Wisconsin was 18,0000; in 1842 it was 42,000; in 1845 it was as high as 117,000, according to the estimate by counties made by members of the legislature; and, in 1846, it was over 150,000. I have heard that this year the population will increase by about 50,000, and this does not seem at all improbable, when we consider the steady stream from the East, not only of immigrants but of Americans as well. Under such circumstances one can easily imagine what a spirited sale there must be of government land priced at $1.25 per acre. I recently saw an account of the receipts at the Milwaukee land office for one week. They amounted to $175,000! Just now the fall immigration by way of Milwaukee is beginning, and a recent issue of a newspaper of that city reports that every steamship brings so many newcomers that they could make quite a respectable little town of their own. The newspaper says it is amusing to watch them go up through the streets in great throngs and it compares them to the tribes of Israel on their entry into the Promised Land. I, too, saw a group of them moving along, in grand confusion, with their heavily loaded wagons, and I think the comparison is very apt. . . .

The next day, which was Sunday, a driver called for us in the morning with a coach drawn by two horses, and after a drive of a couple of hours towards the southwest we arrived at the Norwegian settlement at Muskego Lake. The first people whom we met were a couple from Tinn, both of whom seemed greatly pleased with the visit. True-hearted and simple, just as we find our countrymen here and there up among the mountains in Norway, they had preserved their customs, dress, and general arrangement of the house unchanged, as well as their language. They served us with excellent milk and whatever else they had; and, when they had become confident that we were altogether Norwegian, they also brought some excellent flatbrod, made of wheat which they had at first held back because "these Yankees" are so ready to make fun of it. The Yankee who was with us, however, seemed very well pleased when we let him try it. On a later occasion we induced him to try another dish, just as Norwegian and just as unfamiliar to him, namely fløtegrøt which he declared first-rate as he licked his lips. Our friends from Tinn were well satisfied with their condition; they had managed so well during the first four years that they had paid off the debt they had incurred and now they already had a little surplus.

We next visited, among others, Even Heg, who seems to be one of the leaders among the Norwegians in these parts. He has earned the gratitude of the Norwegians in Wisconsin by starting a printing establishment on his own farm, with the assistance of Mr. Bache, a financier from Drammen. Here they publish the Norwegian-Wisconsin newspaper, Nordlyset, edited by Mr. Reymert. It is without doubt a very good idea through such a medium to maintain a cultural link between the Norwegians here and the mother country, as well as among themselves. Everyone, indeed, who would like to see them preserve their national characteristics and their memories of their native land as long as possible must, first and foremost, turn his attention to the problem of preserving their language by keeping it constantly before their eyes and ears.

I have been greatly interested in finding out how far the Norwegians have progressed in their understanding of American affairs; for example, as to the differences between the political parties. I must say I believe they have not reached beyond the first rudiments of a republican education. To be sure, I shall not lay too much stress on the fact that a couple of them called the government price on land "the king's price," because it would be stretching the point a bit to charge a mere thoughtless expression to their political ignorance.

On the other hand, there are undoubtedly not a few to whom can be applied what an American told me of one whom he had asked if he were a Whig or a Democrat. The American had soon discovered after questioning the Norwegian about the meaning of the terms, and particularly about what he had against the Whig doctrine concerning banks and the protection of industry, that the man did not have the least idea that these matters were the main issues involved in the political struggle. If he had been asked not if he were a Democrat, with which expression he is well acquainted from his home country, but if he were a Locofoco, he would presumably at once have admitted his inability to answer. . . .

I have already suggested how desirable it would be for the Norwegians to see their language frequently in a purer form, not only in their religious literature, but otherwise as well. I had in mind particularly the great ease with which they learn the English language and, unfortunately, the equal facility they have in forgetting their own as soon as they cease to use it every day.

They do not bother about keeping the two languages separate, so that they may speak Norwegian to their own countrymen and English to others; instead they eliminate one word after the other from their Norwegian and substitute English words in such a way that the Norwegian will soon be completely forgotten.

Such a practice, to be sure, is rather common among uneducated people who emigrate to a foreign country, but the Norwegians seem to have a special knack at it. The first words they forget are "ja" and "nei," and, even if everything else about them, from top to toe, is Norwegian, you may be sure they will answer "yes" or "no" if you ask them any questions. Gradually other English words, pertaining to their daily environment, are added. They have a "faens" about their farm and have probably "digget" a well near the house so that they need not go so far to get water to use on their "stoven." Such a well is generally necessary, even if there is a "laek" or a "river" in the vicinity, because such water is generally too warm. Near the houses there is frequently a little garden, where they grow "pompuser" (pumpkins) among other things, and a little beyond is "fila" (the English word "field" with the genuine Norwegian feminine article "a").

The ease with which the Norwegians learn the English language has attracted the attention of the Americans, all the more because they are altogether too ready to consider them entirely raw when they come here. "Never," one of them told me a few days ago, "have I known people to become civilized so rapidly as your countrymen; they come here in motley crowds, dressed up with all kinds of dingle-dangle just like the Indians. But just look at them a year later: they speak English perfectly, and, as far as dress, manners, and ability are concerned, they are quite above reproach."

On the other hand he did not seem to know a great deal about the Norwegians in this country. My impression, after many visits extending over a number of settlements, is that the great mass of the families have essentially changed very little. I shall not deny, however, that they have been able to meet the severe strain of the work with an iron will, and thus have had ample opportunity to strengthen their moral courage. It also seems a fact that there is less drinking here than in Norway, although there are enough drunkards here, too, and among them some who have acquired the habit since they came. Cleanliness is, here as in Norway, for many almost an unheard of thing. The entrance to one of the houses I visited was guarded by a formidable cesspool. If a place looks really filthy and disreputable, you must expect to meet either Norwegians or Swiss or Irish.

Of course there are some notable exceptions, but, on the whole, one must admit that it is among young people who have gone into the service of Americans that one finds that real desire for improvement which makes the Norwegian name respected and almost loved here. This has given our people such a general reputation for respectability, morality, sobriety, and natural ability that I frequently hear expressions to the effect that the whole of Norway might well come here and be received with open arms.

I must add, that among all the people I have talked with I have found very few who said they were dissatisfied and wanted to return to Norway, and with some of these it was more a matter of talk than a real desire to go. And it is not strange if there are some who have been ruined through their emigration. The emigration fever spread through our country districts like a disease, paying no heed to age or sex, rich or poor, the diligent worker or the lazy good-for-nothing. Naturally, many have emigrated who are totally unfit for the strenuous life here, which calls for so much energy, common sense, and endurance if one is to succeed. It is equally true that many have made a mistake in buying or claiming land before they had either the necessary understanding or means to proceed with its cultivation. The fact that there have not been more wrecks than there have, in view of all the mistakes made, gives evidence both of the inherent strength of character of our people and of the excellence of the country itself.

I do not mean to imply that few complaints are heard. Quite the contrary. In addition to the fact that many, indeed most, admit that they had expected the land to be far better than it actually proved to be and that they had been fooled, to some extent, by the false reports contained in letters, there are many other complaints; but all of them are of such a nature that time and habit will presumably remedy the situation. Some complain that the work is too strenuous, others that there is so much ungodliness, others that there is too much sickness.

Practically all the Norwegians have been sick, some of them as much as a year at a time, and this misfortune has hampered many. The daily newspapers are half filled with all kinds of quack advertisements of pills and marvelous medicines against fever and ague and bilious fever; and a certain Dr. Champion drove by here most ostentatiously the other day with two huge boxes of pills. I do not believe there is any other country on earth where sound, healthy people use as much medicine as here, for the prevention of disease. The worst complaint of all is homesickness; everyone experiences that, of course. But time can heal even deeper wounds than that of having been severed from one's native land. . . .

In 1846, Eric Janson, the leader of a pietistic sect in Sweden, founded a communitarian colony at Bishop Hill in Illinois. The two selections that follow, written by settlers at Bishop Hill, offer differing views of the so-called "New Jerusalem."
(Source: Letter From Anders Jonsson in Hudikswalls-Weckoblad, July 17, 1847; Letter From O. Bäck in Norrlands-Posten, March 31, 1849.)

I take pen in hand, moved by the Holy Ghost, to bear witness to the things I have seen, heard, and experienced. We had a pleasant voyage . . . and I was not affected in the least with seasickness . . . . My words are inadequate to describe with what joy we are permitted daily to draw water from the well of life and how we have come to the land of Canaan, flowing with milk and honey, . . . which the Scriptures tell us the Lord has prepared for his people. He has brought us out of the devilish bondage of the ecclesiastical authorities, which still holds you in captivity . . . . Here we are relieved of hearing and seeing Sweden's satellites of the devil, whose tongues are inspired by the minions of hell and who murdered the prophets and Jesus himself and snatched the Bible from Eric Janson's hands and came against us with staves, guns, and torches, together with ropes and chains, to take away the freedom we have in Christ. But praised by God through all eternity that we are freed from them and are now God's peculiar people . . . . This is the land of liberty, where everybody can worship God in his own way and can choose pastors who are full of the Spirit, light, and perfection . . . . Therefore, make ready and let nothing hinder you . . . and depart from Babel, that is, Sweden, fettered body and soul by the law . . . .

Janson is a rich man. He has fifty teams of horses, twenty yoke of oxen, three hundred cows, three hundred and three sheep, four hundred slaves, one judge, a bookkeeper, a foreman, a gamekeeper, and twelve apostles. Of the total number of emigrants, only three hundred are alive, and one hundred of them have deserted in favor of the new towns that have sprung up. He has more than three hundred hogs, and I do not know how many chickens, geese, ducks, and turkeys, but there are many . . . . He has sent many loads of wheat to Chicago, Rock Island, and Peoria . . . and still only a few months ago his people were compelled to live on the bread of sorrow and mush, that is, a mixture of corn and potatoes. Also, through the winter the people have threshed for him and the Americans and have earned a great amount of wheat. He has purchased a threshing machine, which is loaded on two wagons and drawn by two horses from place to place. He can thresh at least one hundred and fifty bushels per day and demands every third bushel for his services, and still the people have to live on a miserable diet . . . . To the victims of severe sickness he says, "You are damned because you have not faith; you must descend into hell with your apostasy . . . ." Every conceivable form of disease and misery has come upon these people . . . .

A PROTOTYPE OF AN "AMERICA LETTER"---1850

The following selection, a letter from Johan Johansson of Burlington, Iowa, may be considered a prototype of all the "America Letters" that Swedish immigrants were sending back to the Old Country. Although only an excerpt, one can see the attention paid to details, as well as the deep-seated dissatisfaction with Swedish society, institutions and government. (Source: Letter from Johan Johansson in Östgotha Correspondenten, April 15, 1850.)

Tell Johannes . . . and others not to condemn me for failing to return home at the appointed time, as I promised and intended when I left Sweden, because at that time I was as ignorant as the other stay-at-homes about what a voyage to a foreign land entails. When a person is abroad in the world, there may be many changes in health and disposition, but if God grants me health I will come when it pleases me. If it were not for the sake of my good mother and my relatives, I would never return to Sweden. No one need worry about my circumstances in America, because I am living on God's noble and free soil, neither am I a slave under others. On the contrary, I am my own master, like the other creatures of God. I have now been on American soil for two and a half years and I have not been compelled to pay a penny for the privilege of living. Neither is my cap worn out from lifting it in the presence of gentlemen. There is no class distinction here between high and low, rich and poor, no make-believe, no "title sickness," or artificial ceremonies, but everything is quiet and peaceful and everybody lives in peace and prosperity. Nobody goes from door to door begging crumbs.

. . . The Americans do not have to scrape their effects together and sell them in order to pay heavy taxes to the crown and to pay the salaries of officials. There are no large estates, whose owners can take the last sheaf from their dependents and then turn them out to beg. Neither is a drink of brännvin forced on the workingman in return for a day's work . . . I sincerely hope that nobody in Sweden will foolishly dissuade anyone from coming to this land of Canaan . . . .

PINE LAKE: AN UNSUCCESSFUL COLONY---1850

Fredrika Bremer, the famous Swedish author, visited the various Scandinavian settlements of the mid-west in 1849-1850. In a book that she wrote a few years later, she vividly described the places she had visited, and the Scandinavian immigrants she had observed. One colony, the unsuccessful Pine Lake Settlement of Gustaf Unonius, caused her to write this dismal report.
(Source: Fredrika Bremer, Homes of the New World, Stockholm, Sweden, 1853.)

The little Swedish colony at Pine Lake, although scattered, still contains half a dozen families who live as farmers in the neighborhood . . . . Almost all of them live in log cabins and appear to have scant means. The most prosperous is a blacksmith, who has built himself a lovely frame house in the woods. Bergvall is also prosperous. In Sweden he had been a member of the gentry, but here he is a practical farmer and has obtained several acres of good land which he works with much industry and perseverance. He seems well, and has retained his happy optimistic Swedish nature. Another member of the original colony who had managed to hold on was B. Peterson, a shoemaker . . . .Here on a high promontory, covered with gleaming masses of leaves, the New Uppsala was to be built. That was what Unonius and his friend planned when they first came into the wilderness and were delighted with its beauty. Alas! the wild soil would not support old Uppsala's sons. I saw the deserted houses where he Unonius and Von Schneidau in vain fought poverty and tried to live . . . .

The lot of Scandinavian women in the settlements of the middle-west was particularly hard. Fredrika Bremer recorded the picture of a lonely Norwegian woman who had migrated from Norway to the Koshkonong settlement in Wisconsin.

(Source: Fredrika Bremer, <u>Homes of the New World</u>, Stockholm, Sweden, 1853.)

The Norwegian pastor, Mr. P [reus] had only left Norway to come hither a few months before. His young and pretty wife was standing in the kitchen, where a fire was blazing, boiling groats as I entered. I accosted her in Swedish. She was amazed at first, and terrified by the late visit, as her husband was from home on an official journey, and she was here quite alone with her little brother and an old woman servant; but she received us with true Northern hospitality and good-will, and she was ready to do everything in the world to entertain and accommodate us . . . . She was only 19, sick at heart for her mother, her home, and the mountains of her native land, nor was she happy in this strange country, and in those new circumstances to which she was so little accustomed. She was pretty, refined, and graceful; her whole appearance, her dress, her guitar which hung on the wall, everything showed that she had lived in a sphere very different to that of a log-house in a wilderness, and among rude peasants. The house was not in good condition; it rained in through the roof. Her husband, to whom she had not long been married, and whom for love she had accompanied from Norway to the New World, had been now from home for several days; she had neither friend nor acquaintance near nor far in the new hemisphere. It was no wonder that she was unable to see any thing beautiful or excellent in "this disagreeable America." But a young creature, good and lovely as she is, will not long remain lonely among the warm-hearted people of this country.

In addition to her book, Fredrika Bremer also wrote a series of "America Letters," which were also very persuasive in motivating Scandinavian emigration to America. The one quoted here, is probably the most famous of all the letters sent back to Scandinavia by this renowned author.

(Source: Adolph B. Benson, America of the Fifties, Letter of Fredrika Bremer, New York, 1924.)

I asked many, both men and women, whether they were contented--- whether they were better off here than in old Norway. Nearly all of them replied, "Yes, we are better off here; we do not work so hard, and it is easier to gain a livelihood." One old peasant said, "There are difficulties here as well as there. The health is better in the old country than here!"

I visited . . . some of the Norwegian peasant houses. The Norwegians wisely built their houses beside some little brook or river and understood how to select a good soil. They came thither as old and accustomed agriculturists and knew how to make use of the ground. They help one another in their labor, live frugally, and ask for no pleasures. The land seems to me . . . to be rich and has an idyllic beauty. Mountains there are none; only swelling hills crowned with pinewood . . . .

Every year brings new immigrants, and they often settle upon tracts of land very distant from other colonists . . . .

Wisconsin is a state for agriculture and the rearing of cattle; the land in many parts, however, and in particular around Madison, where it is appropriated by the Federal government for supplying an income to the State University, is already very dear. It has been purchased by speculators at the government price, a dollar and a quarter per acre, and resold by them for not less than ten or twelve dollars per acre. "And who will give so much for it?" I inquired of Chancellor Lathrop. "Your countrymen," he replied quickly. "Your countrymen. Whose sons will be freely educated at our University."

Oct. 1850, in Minnesota. This Minnesota is a glorious country, and just the country for Northern emigrants--- just the country for a new Scandinavia. It is four times as large as England; its soil is of the richest description, with extensive wooded tracts; great number of rivers and lakes abounding in fish, and a healthy, invigorating climate. The winters are cold and clear; the summers not so hot as in those states lying lower on the Mississippi . . . .

What a glorious new Scandinavia might not Minnesota become! Here the Swede would find again his clear, romantic lakes, the plains of Scone rich in corn, and the valleys of Norrland; here the Norwegian would find his rapid rivers, his lofty mountains, for I include the Rocky Mountains and Oregon in the new kingdom; and both nations, their hunting-fields and their fisheries. The Danes might here pasture their flocks and herds, and lay out their farms on richer and less misty coasts than those of Denmark .

. . .Yet seriously, Scandinavians who are well off in the Old Country ought not to leave it. But such as are too much contracted at home, and who desire to emigrate, should come to Minnesota . . . .

113

The following selection is an excerpt from the autobiography of
Phineas T. Barnum, the great nineteenth century impressario. It describes his bringing to the United States, the great Swedish musical star,
Jenny Lind, who, in addition to her musical talents, was a generous phil-
anthropist. She always was willing, by concerts or direct gifts of money,
to aid her Swedish immigrant brethren who had come to America.
(Source: P.T. Barnum, Life, New York, 1855.)

. . . . In October, 1849, I first conceived the idea of bringing Jenny
Lind to this country. I had never heard her sing . . . . Her reputation,
however, was sufficient for me. I usually jump at conclusions, and almost
invariably find that my first impressions are the most correct. It struck
me, when I first thought of this speculation, that if properly managed it
must prove immensely profitable, provided I could engage the "Swedish
Nightingale" on any terms within the range of reason. As it was a great
undertaking, I considered the matter seriously for several days, and all
my "cipherings" and calculations gave but one result---immense success. .
. . . I may as well here state, that although I relied prominently upon
Jenny Lind's reputation as a great musical artiste, I also took largely into
my estimate of her success with all classes of the American public, her
character for extraordinary benevolence and generosity. Without this
peculiarity in her disposition, I never would have dared make the engage-
ment which I did, as I felt sure that there were multitudes of individuals
in America who would be prompted to attend her concerts by this feeling
alone.

Thousands of persons covered the shipping and piers, and other thousands had congregated on the wharf at Canal Street, to see her. The wildest enthusiasm prevailed as the noble steamer approached the dock . . . .
A superb bower of green trees, decorated with beautiful flags, was discovered upon the wharf, together with two triumphal arches, on one of
which was inscribed, "Welcome, Jenny Lind!" The second was surmounted
by the American eagle, and bore the inscription, "Welcome to America!"
These decorations were probably not produced by magic, and I do not know
that I can reasonably find fault with some persons who suspected that I
had a hand in their erection . . . .

Jenny Lind's first concert was fixed to come off at Castle Garden on
Wednesday evening, September 11, and most of the tickets were sold at
auction on the Saturday and Monday previous to the concert. Genin the
hatter laid the foundation of his fortune by purchasing the first ticket at
$225.

The proprietors of the Garden saw fit to make the usual charge of
one shilling to all persons who entered the premises, yet three thousand
persons were present at the auction. One thousand tickets were sold
on the first day for an aggregate sum of $10,141 . . . .

The reception of Jenny Lind on her first appearance, in point of enthusiasm, was probably never before equaled in the world. As Mr. Benedict led her towards the foot-lights, the entire audience rose to their feet
and welcomed her with three cheers, accompanied by the waving of thou-

sands of hats and handkerchiefs.   This was by far the largest audience that
Jenny had ever sung before.   She was evidently much agitated, but the orchestra commenced, and before she had sung a dozen notes of "Casta Diva,"
she began to recover her self-possession, and long before the scene was
concluded, she was as calm as if sitting in her own drawing-room.   Towards the last portion of the cavatina, the audience were so completely
carried away by their feelings, that the remainder of the air was drowned
in a perfect tempest of acclamation.   Enthusiasm had been wrought to its
highest pitch, but the musical powers of Jenny Lind exceeded all the brilliant anticipations which had been formed, and her triumph was complete . . .

It would seem as if the Jenny Lind mania had reached its culminating
point before hearing her, and I confess that I feared the anticipations of
the public were too high to be realized, and hence that there would be a
reaction after the first concert, but I was happily disappointed.   The trans-
cendent musical genius of the Swedish Nightingale was superior to all the
pictures which fancy could paint, and the furore did not attain its highest
point until she had been heard.   The people were in ecstasies; the powers
of editorial acumen, types and ink, were inadequate to sound her praises.
The Rubicon was passed . . . .

The great assembly at Castle Garden was not gathered by Jenny
Lind's great musical genius and powers alone.   She was effectually brought
before the public before they had seen or heard her.   She appeared in the
presence of a jury already excited to enthusiasm in her behalf.   She more
than met their expectations, and all the means I had adopted to prepare the
way were thus abundantly justified.

As a manager, I worked by setting others to work.   Biographies of
the Swedish Nightingale were largely circulated; "Foreign Correspondence"
glorified her talents and triumphs by narratives of her benevolence; and
"printer's ink" was employed, in every possible form, to put and keep
Jenny Lind before the people.

The following is an extract of a letter written by a Swedish immigrant in Chicago, describing the plight of his countrymen in this growing metropolis of the midwest.

(Source: Augustana Historical Society Publications, VII, Rock Island, Illinois, 1937.)

Chicago, Illinois, September 20, 1852.

This year we have had a dreadful situation in Chicago, caused by the great number of Swedish emigrants who have come here destitute, and during the unhealthful season. It is strange that in spite of the very low altitude, Chicago seems to have become a more healthful place year by year; but it usually, nay, always, happens that the unhealthful season always begins with the coming of the emigrants. This summer we had the most healthful weather, and everyone spoke of the freshness and healthfulness of the season, until the arrival of a detachment of Swedes who were housed too many to a room (there is always a scarcity of houses and rooms to rent in spite of the great amount of building every year). In one of these houses cholera broke out. In a five-room house (three rooms on the first floor and two on the second) there lived in the largest room, about twelve by sixteen, a man and wife with their five children; in the next room a grandmother and a man and wife with three children; in another a man and wife with two children and another man; in another a man, wife, and five children; and in the smallest a mother and two children, altogether twenty-eight people, of whom fifteen died in one week. Among the survivors were six orphaned children. After a few days the sickness declined, but it increased again when the next group of Swedish emigrants arrived. Thus it has been for the last two months. Of those who come here about one third are destitute, without a cent, with only some old clothes and trash; one third, perhaps, have a few dollars; and those who have more usually go farther west to buy land, so you can imagine that Chicago is full of Swedish beggars. And who is there to help them? That has been my job since I first came here with the Jansonists a few years ago. As a punishment for not "believing" the teachings of the prophet, some of them were transported like cattle and put on half rations; they took sick and complained, and for this reason the prophet's assistants disowned them as children of the devil and left them here starving and ruined. Since that time an ever-increasing number of emigrants have needed my help. This year there seems to be more poor people than ever. I have had to give all my time to providing shelter and food for them through my friends and others. L. is beside herself from the crying and wailing in our house, where they come every day with their tales of woe. L. distributes among them the contents of a barrel of flour, salt meat, rice, which, including other articles of food, are kept purposely for them; but often they have no means of preparing the food and no house to live in, and then in damp and rainy weather it is pretty hard to see mothers with infants in their arms and other children hanging on to their skirts complaining of hunger and cold. Added to this is their ignorance of the language, so they can not take one step alone and are unable to get work, because no one wants a person who cannot understand what he is told to do.
. . . .

116

OLE BULL AND HIS OLEANA COLONY---1853

In 1853, Ditmar Meidell, a Norwegian newspaper editor, wrote a satirical ballad entitled, "Oleana", as a thrust at the exaggerated claims made by the great Norwegian violinist, Ole Bull, for his American colony in Pennsylvania, which ultimately proved to be an unsuccessful venture. That poem is quoted here.

(Source: Ditmar Meidell, Oleana, Norway, 1853; verse translation by Theodore C. Blegen in, Studies and Records of the Norwegian---American Historical Association II, Northfield, Minnesota, 1927, 117-121.)

I'm off to Oleana, I'm turning from my doorway,
No - chains - for - me, I'll say good-bye to slavery in Norway.
Ole---Ole---Ole---oh! Oleana!
Ole---Ole---Ole---oh! Oleana!

They give you land for nothing in jolly Oleana,
And grain comes leaping from the ground in floods of golden manna.

The grain it does the threshing, it pours into the sack, Sir,
And so you take a quiet nap a-stretching on your back, Sir.

The crops they are gigantic, potatoes are immense, Sir,
You make a quart of whisky from each one without expense, Sir.

And ale as strong and sweet as the best you've ever tasted,
It's running in the foamy creek, where most of it is wasted.

The salmon they are playing, and leaping in the brook, Sir,
They hop into your kettle, put the cover on, and cook, Sir.

And little roasted piggies, with manners quite demure, Sir,
They ask you, "Will you have some ham?" And then you say, "Why
    sure, Sir."

The cows are most obliging, their milk they put in pails, Sir,
They make your cheese and butter with a skill that never fails, Sir.

The bull he is the master, his calves he likes to boss, Sir,
He beats them when they loaf about, he's never at a loss, Sir.

The calves are helpful, themselves they skin and kill, Sir,
They turn into a tasty roast before you drink your fill, Sir.

The hens lay eggs colossal, so big and round and fine, Sir,
The roosters act like eight-day clocks, they always tell the time, Sir.

And cakes come raining down, Sir, with chocolate frosting coated,
They're nice and rich and sweet, good Lord, you eat them till you're
    bloated.

And all night long, the sun shines, it always keeps a-glowing,
It gives you eyes just like a cat's to see where you are going.

The moon is also beaming, it's always full, I vow Sir,
A bottle for a telescope, I'm looking at it now, Sir.

Two dollars for carousing they give each day, and more, Sir,
For if your good and lazy, they will even give you four, Sir.

Support your wife and kids? Why the country pays for that, Sir,
You'd slap officials down and out if they should leave you flat, Sir.

And if you've any bastards, you're freed of their support, Sir,
As you can guess since I'm spinning verses for your sport, Sir.

You walk about in velvet, with silver buttons bright, Sir,
You puff away at meerschaum pipes, your women pack them right, Sir.

The dear old ladies struggle, and sweat for us and labor,
And if they're cross, they spank themselves, they do it as a favor.

And so we play the fiddle, and all of us are glad, Sir,
We dance a merry polka, boys, and that is not so bad, Sir.

I'm off to Oleana to lead a life of pleasure,
A beggar here, a count out there, with riches in full measure.

    I'm coming Oleana, I've left my native doorway,
    I've made my choice, I've said goodbye to slavery in Norway.
    Ole---Ole---Ole---Oh! Oleana!
    Ole---Ole---Ole---Oh! Oleana!

It did not take the Oleana colonists long to discover that the settlement was something less than Utopia. The first selection cited here is an excerpt from a letter by one of the settlers, Jacob Olsen Wollaug, who recorded his disallusionment with Oleana; the second selection is a portion of a letter written by Ole Bull, himself, to his brother explaining his hopes and dreams for the colony he was attempting to establish.
(Source: Christiania-Posten, May 25, 1853; Christiania-Posten, June 14, 1853.)(Blegen, Norwegian Migration to America, Northfield, Minnesota, 1931.)

Upon our arrival at New York on September 11, we were engaged to go to Mr. Ole Bull's new colony in Pennsylvania, where all were to get work at a half dollar and board per day or a dollar a day without board; artisans were to receive more---from three-fourths to one dollar and board. Everyone could select land to suit himself, from twenty-five acres, at three dollars per acre, to be paid for in three years at the rate of two dollars a month. Bull was to furnish all necessaries, such as houses and the like, against a monthly reimbursement . . . .

Upon our arrival we found ourselves disappointed in our expectations, for the land looked very miserable to us. The road to the colony, which is situated about ten Norwegian miles from the railroad, was very poor and grew worse the farther we went, until at the end we found ourselves in the midst of high mountains and narrow valleys cut by small rivers and streams, with heavy forests . . . so that everyone understood that it would take a generation here to clear a farm or gaard that would adequately support a family . . . .

Of my activity as an artist, politician, and manager of my little state in Pennsylvania, you can form a conception only when you learn that I am simultaneously laying out five towns and making a contract with the government for the casting of some 10,000 cannons in Oleana for the forts, especially those in California. I have succeeded in getting Philadelphia to subscribe two million dollars to the Sunbury and Erie Road, which will go near the colony on the south; New York has also subscribed two millions to a branch of the Erie and New York Railroad from Elmira to Oleana to run through the northern part of the colony so that Oleana will be only twelve hours from New York, ten hours from Philadelphia, and about eleven hours from Baltimore . . . .

You ask me how I could have got all this in operation, how I can, so to speak, play with millions. Good Edward, when you see for yourself you will be much more surprised; this is merely a beginning; my powers have grown proportionately with the magnitude of the work; my enthusiasm has triumphed over skepticism. My persecutors have themselves called into play my indisputable right to defend myself, and I answer with facts!

The work of Swedish clergymen among the many Scandinavian immigrants in the United States was of more than ordinary import. The Reverend Erland Carlsson of the Swedish Lutheran Church, who served in America for twenty-two years, rendered invaluable services not only to the Swedish Lutheran Church, but to others of his countrymen, regardless of their religious affiliation. Chicago was the clearing house of immigration, and it was said that Carlsson's home was a miniature Castle Garden. In a letter, Carlsson gives a graphic picture of a typical day in his life. (Source: Letter From Erland Carlsson in Nya Wexjö--Bladet, April 13, 1855.) in Augustana Historical Society Publications, V, Rock Island, Illinois, 1932.)

If our work as pastors here were judged by the membership of our congregations, it might be thought that we are not very busy. But everything is new here. Congregations must be organized; constitutions adopted; by-laws drawn up; churches built, etc. Besides, duties are increased tenfold by the multitudes who are carried with the stream of emigration through this city or who reside here a few months. They are unable to rent a room, obtain employment, consult a physician, etc., without assistance, and usually it is the pastor who is called upon. The reason for this is that they are unfamiliar with the language. But even though they have learned enough to get along in everyday affairs, they are, nevertheless, helpless when business is transacted, a contract drawn up, a bill of exchange sent to Sweden or cashed---in all such matters the pastor must stand ready to help. Add to this the fact that from east to west letters are addressed to him. Sometimes I have brought with me to church more than fifty letters. Then there are scores of letters containing every conceivable kind of inquiries to be answered. Moreover, the pastor must take part in secular activities, and I have fully as many of them as any pastor in the most populous parish in Sweden. I keep office hours from 8 to 10 a.m. and from 2 to 3 p.m., and people ordinarily come in a constant stream. It is seldom that I am left alone at the other hours. I am teaching English to a class of children a few hours a week. I am instructing confirmands at two places: twelve in St. Charles and twenty in Chicago. Under the weight of so many burdens not only does one become fatigued physically and mentally, but there is danger of destroying the life of the spirit . . . . Our churches are filled with attentive listeners, and the number of members has materially increased in more recent times. I have six congregations under my care, which I visit regularly every month. When congregations are organized, it is necessary to build churches; and that is no easy problem . . . .

While most of the "America Letters" sent back to Norway were glowing descriptions of the United States, occassionally, a letter or two was not full of cheerful and naive optimism. The following letter written by a Norwegian settler in Wisconsin in 1857 provides one of these rare examples. (Source: Richard B. Eide, (comp.) and ed., Norse Immigrant Letters: Glimpses of Norse Immigrant Life in the Northwest in the Fifties, Minneapolis, 1925.)

Dear Friend and Cousin:

I have received your most welcome letter which in part pleases me and in part causes me much pain. You will perhaps wonder why I say it pains me, but the reason is that I see that you, with your little ones, intend to come over here. If you can stay at home and in some way make your living, you must retain your farm and never think of coming to America.

In the first place, the journey across the ocean is so difficult that one can hardly endure it, and if you should live through it and land, where, then, would you go? Certainly everything would be strange, even the language. A farm for a small family like yours, costs at least $800, for land has raised in price during late years. If you should buy farm implements much more money would be needed and yet your stock would be comparatively small . . . .

The winter here is shorter than that in Norway, but it is usually much colder, and when summer comes, that in turn, is much warmer. Our minister told me that the heat this week has been between 88 and 94 degrees, so you see it is very hard to endure the labor that is necessary under such conditions. Many people not adjusted to the climate break down.

If you still do not give up the idea of coming to America, kindly write me as soon as possible in order that I might be of as much help to you as possible. But yet, I must, as I have already said, urge as a friend and relative, that you never think any more about this journey. I will tell you straightforwardly that I hardly think that you will have enough money left, after you arrive here, with which to buy land, and if you should go as far as Iowa before buying land where it is said that land may be had---then all that you may have would not suffice to pay the journey's expense, since travel by railroad and stage coach has in late years become much more expensive. I might also say that various kinds of diseases often attack newcomers. Among these, the fever is the worst. I, too was in bed for sixteen weeks at one time because of this sickness, and although I have often been troubled with it since this time, others have suffered much more . . . I hope that the information I have given you will help you in deciding to think no more of coming to America.

In 1861, the first Norwegian-American college in the United States, Luther College, opened its doors. It has sometimes been grandeliquently called the "Norwegian University". From the memoirs of an English farmer who lived in Decorah, Iowa, we see some aspects of college life through the eyes of a non-Norwegian observer.
(Source: Harcourt H. Horn, An English Colony in Iowa, Boston, 1931.)

A fine Luther College . . . stood on a hill overlooking the town. It had a strong faculty, headed by a president of marked ability. They turned out well educated scholars, many of whom have made names for themselves in the literary and scholastic world. The students organized a glee club, giving public recitals, which brought forth generous applause, especially those parts which were rendered without instrumental accompaniment, in which they certainly did excel.... The professors of the Norwegian Luther College, with their wives, were constant visitors [at the town skating rink], skating perhaps with a little more sedateness than the students.

. . .The students of course were in their element, and figures of eight, the outside edge backwards, and similar movements not easily acquired by the tyro, were executed by them as a mere matter of routine.

Undoubtedly the most graceful and daring skater was the daughter of the principal of the College. She was always the centre of attraction . . . . My wife used to call on her mother at the College, always meeting with a kindly welcome, accompanied by the appearance of cake and wine.

AN AMERICAN CONSUL'S DILEMMA---1863

With the outbreak of the Civil War, thousands of young men in Sweden and Norway flocked to the office of the American consul, and attempted to volunteer for the Union Army, hoping in this way to get free passage across the Atlantic. The American consul at Stockholm, B.F. Tefft, described this perplexing problem in a report dated January 9, 1863.

(Source: Reports From the Consuls of the United States, vol. 12, No. 76, 1865.)

My office is overrun with applicants, from Sweden and Norway, who wish to go to the United States and enter the Army . . . .

Had I the means of sending such applicants to America, I believe I could send a thousand a month for a year or two to come. I have had, sometimes from ten to twenty Swedish and Norwegian soldiers, with their uniforms upon them, together seeking a way to get to America for the above purpose . . . .

What shall I do in relation to these numerous, increasing, and altogether troublesome applications?

As Swedish immigrants continued to arrive at the port of New York, the Augustana Synod felt the need to establish a religious mission in that city to aid the new comers. The following is a portion of a letter by Reverend Hasselquist describing the early history of the New York mission. (Source: Letter from Reverend Hasselquist, January 18, 1866, in Augustana Historical Society Publications, II, Rock Island, Illinois, 1932.)

The Augustana Synod has for a long time known that a large number of our countrymen resided in the city of New York and in other places in the eastern states; often have we considered by what ways and means we should begin spiritual work among them, but we have not felt able to undertake it for want of resources and also of laborers, who are so greatly needed in the West.   Although Ev. Fosterlandsstiftelsen with brotherly love has offered to assist us by paying the greater part of the salary, we could not spare a suitable person, as our field here, already too large for our man-power, is ever expanding.

The necessity, however, of beginning this mission has every year seemed greater and greater; hence the synod at its last meeting in June 1865 felt that it could no longer delay this matter and therefore instructed its committee on Home Missions in the name of the Lord to call Rev. A. Andreen without delay to take up missionary work in New York.

He readily accepted this appointment and has already been at this post during four months. His experiences have still further proved to us, if further proof were required, that the need was greater than we had supposed. As all beginning is difficult, we requested Rev. E. Carlsson to accompany Brother Andreen, and with his rich experience, gathered during many years in Chicago, to assist him on their arrival in New York. This arrangement also had the effect that the cause attracted more attention and aroused interest. Through Rev. Carlsson's efforts several obstacles were overcome, so that they obtained the right of admission to Castle Garden, enabling them to meet the emigrants, as they landed. Several other privileges were also procured for the benefit of the emigrants with reference to the continuation of their journey.

"At the first services there were gathered about 200 people. Some came out of curiosity; yet there were still more, who had heard nothing at all of our services, and who, one by one, had to be sought out in their homes.

"We found that in the city there lived a great number of our countrymen, of whom comparatively very few had been willing to join other church groups; several who had felt constrained to do this, on account of the lack of the proclaiming of the Word of God in accordance with our old confession, are laboring with much love and sacrifice both of time and means for the success of our undertaking.

A Swede, Pehrson, who had studied at a Lutheran College in this country, and been ordained by the so-called Melanchthon Synod, has indeed diligently toiled to build up a congregation, but without much success. It can therefore be stated, that the greater number of the Swedes were without any church connection, and hence exposed to all the evil influences.

124

which a large commercial city carries with it; they were waiting and longing that something would be done for them.   Many have no doubt been lost
not only to our church but to heaven, in consequence of the fact that the
Word of God in which they had been instructed had not been preached to
them in their native tongue.

However, a Swedish congregation has been organized, and chose the
name Gustavus Adolphus.   The trustees are men of esteem and prestige
in the whole city, not to say in the whole country.   They have also displayed a laudable zeal for the congregation and its future; through their
efforts a commodious church has been purchased for $17,000, of which
amount members of the church, and, I believe, mainly the trustees, contributed $3,000.   The first Swedish service was celebrated there the
Third Sunday in Advent.   Thus, God be praised, we now possess a church
home in the great city of New York . . . .

A STATE IMMIGRATION COMMISSIONER---1867

Hans Mattson, a Swedish immigrant of the 1840's, was appointed General Manager of the Minnesota Immigration Board. In his memoirs, he described his primary functions.
(Source: Hans Mattson, Reminiscences, St. Paul, 1892.)

. . . . One of my first tasks as General Manager was to succor the new settlers along the Minnesota River, which the year before had been afflicted with a severe drought. When that was done, I was instructed to engage Swedish, Norwegian, and German agents and interpreters to meet "our" immigrants in New York and Quebec and then escort them to Minnesota. Information about jobs and land for sale was also to be provided. Next, agreements were made with newspapers in various languages to publish complete articles, composed by myself and others, regarding the State of Minnesota and its natural resources . . . . I also wrote promotion pamphlets, had them printed in Swedish, Norwegian and German, and distributed at railroad stations, on ocean vessals, and within the countries in which the above languages were spoken. They were as correct and informative as possible. And, I have many times, when visiting well-to-do farmers on the western prairies, seen these booklets, carrying my name as author, carefully preserved on the bookshelf with the family Bible, the prayer book, the Lutheran Cathechism, and a few other souvenirs from the old fatherland . . . .

In December, 1868, . . . I set out alone on my first visit to Sweden, after an absence of nearly eighteen years. The chief object of the Journey was recreation and pleasure; the second object to make the resources of Minnesota better known among the farming and laboring classes who had made up their minds to emigrate . . . .

At that time only a few Swedish emigrants had returned from America, and to see a man who had been eighteen years in America, and had been a Colonel in the American army must have been a great curiosity, especially to the country people; for wherever it was known that I would pass, people flocked from their houses to the roads and streets in order to catch a glimpse of the returned traveler. . . .

The new ideas now permeating society in Europe, and which will gradually transform it, have, to a great extent, originated in America, more particularly the idea of brotherhood, the sympathy with equals, the conviction that it is our duty to better the condition of our fellowmen, and not despise them, even if they are unfortunate. In this respect, as well as in many others, America exerts a great influence over Europe. To me the better situated classes of Swedes seem short-sighted in their hostility to emigration, for a man of broad views must admit that emigration has been beneficial to Sweden herself. . . .

As late as the 1870's, the glowing reports contained in the "America Letters" continued to be sent back to the Scandinavian Countries. The following letter, written by Gjert Gregorivssen Hovland to friends in Norway, shows that the content of these documents had changed very little in thirty years.

(Source: Theodore C. Blegen, ed., "A Typical America Letter," Mississippi Valley Historical Review, IX, June, 1922, 71-72.)

I must take this opportunity to let you know that we are in the best of health, and that we---both my wife and I---find ourselves exceedingly satisfied. Our son attends the English school, and talks English as well as the native born. Nothing has made me more happy and contented than the fact that we left Norway and journeyed to this country. We have gained more since our arrival here than I did during all the time that I lived in Norway, and I have every prospect of earning a livelihood here for myself and my family---even if my family were larger---so long as God gives me good health.

Such excellent plans have been developed here that, even though one be infirm, no one need suffer want. Competent men are elected whose duty it is to see that no needy persons, either in the cities or in the country, shall have to beg for their living. If a man dies and is survived by a widow and children who are unable to support themselves---as is so often the case---they have the privilege of petitioning these officials. To each one will then be given every year as much as is needed of clothes and food, and no discrimination will be shown between the native-born and those from foreign countries. These things I have learned through daily observation, and I do not believe there can be better laws and arrangements . . . in the whole world. I have talked with a sensible person who has traveled in many countries, who has lived here twenty-six years, and has a full knowledge of the matter; both of him and of other reliable persons I have made inquiries, for I wish to let everyone know the truth.

When assemblies are held to elect officials who are to serve the country, the vote of the common man carries just as much authority and influence as does that of the rich and powerful man. Neither in the matter of clothes nor in seats are distinctions to be observed, whether one be a farmer or a clerk. The freedom which one enjoys is just as good as that of the other. So long as he comports himself honestly he will be subjected to no interference. Everybody has the liberty to travel about in the country, wherever he wishes, without any passports or papers. Everyone is permitted to engage in whatever business he finds most desirable, in trade or commerce, by land or by water. But if anyone is found guilty of crime, he will be prosecuted and severely punished for it.

No duties are levied upon goods which are produced in the country and brought to the city by water or by land. In case of death, no registration is required; the survivor, after paying the debts, is free to dispose of the property for himself and his family just as he desires ; . . . It would heartily please me if I could learn that every one of you who are in need and have little chance of gaining support for yourselves and your families would make up your mind to leave Norway and come to America, for, even if many more were to come, there would still be room here for all. For all those who are willing to work there is no lack of employment and business here. It is possible for all to live in comfort and without suffering want. I do not believe that any of those who suffer under the oppression of others and who must rear their children under straitened circumstances could do better than to help the latter to come to America. But alas, many persons, even though they want to come, lack the necessary means and many others are so stupid as to believe that it is best to live in the country where they have been brought up even if they have nothing but hard bread to satisfy their hunger. It is as if they should say that those who move to a better land, where there is plenty, commit a wrong. But I can find no place where our Creator has forbidden one to seek one's food in an honorable manner. I should like to talk to many persons in Norway for a little while, but we do not wish to live in Norway. We lived there altogether too long. Nor have I talked with any immigrant in this country who wished to return . . . .

A MONUMENT FOR SWEDISH SETTLERS---1876

In 1876, Senator Thomas Bayard of Delaware, a descendent of the Swedish settlers of the seventeenth century, addressed a letter to the representative of the Swedish government at Washington, explaining the desire of the Historical Society of Delaware to erect a monument to the original Swedish colonists who had inhabited the region that was now the state of Delaware.

(Source: New York Times, March 14, 1876.)

The Historical Society of the State of Delaware, having it in view to commemorate the first landing of the Swedish colonists in Delaware, appointed a commission of eleven persons, of whom I am one, to take the subject into consideration. After due conference, the committee have reported to the Historical Society a resolution to have erected a monument, to be constructed of native granite, and placed within a very short distance of the shore of the River Christiania, and adjacent to the point of rocks upon which the actual disembarkation took place in the year 1632. The ancient church of the Holy Trinity (whose corporate title is the Swede's Lutheran Church) stands nearby, having a plot of ground inclosed within its churchyard walls, a convenient, accessible, and conspicuous portion of which the wardens and vestry have conveyed to the Historical Society as a site for the proposed monument. The Swedish colony whose foundation in this country it is thus proposed to preserve in history was originated in Sweden . . . . The archives of the Swedish government no doubt contain a full and accurate history of the expedition, with the names and numbers of the persons concerned. In this bringing to your attention the essential facts, I would respectfully ask that you cause them to be communicated to your Government and sovereign, and that the Historical Society of Delaware may be informed whether it would be agreeable to the Swedish Government to take part in the proposed monumental commemoration of this interesting event in the annals of both our countries. The countenance and aid of the Swedish Government would be accepted by the Society with sincere gratification and warm acknowledgment . . . .

Among the many propaganda agencies luring immigrants westward during the 1870's and 1880's, none was more effective than the railroad. What follows is a typical circular issued by the Burlington and Missouri River Railroad, that was widely distributed throughout the midwest. Many a Scandinavian immigrant took the bait.
(Source: Richard C. Overton, Burlington West, Cambridge, 1941, p. 345.)

Ho for the West! Nebraska ahead! The truth will out! The best farming and stock raising country in the world! The great central region, not too hot or too cold.

The facts about Western Iowa and Southern Nebraska are being slowly but surely discovered by all intelligent men. The large population now pouring into this region, consists of shrewd and well-informed farmers, who know what is good, and are taking advantage of the opportunities offered.

The crops of Southern Nebraska are as fine as can be; a large wheat and barley crop has been harvested; corn is in splendid condition and all other crops are equally fine. The opportunities now offered to buy B. & M. R. R. lands on long credit, low interest, twenty percent rebate for improvements, low freights and fares, free passes to those who buy, &c., &c., can never again be found.

There are plenty of lands elsewhere, but they are in regions which can never be largely prosperous. Southern Nebraska, with its fine soil, pure water, and moderate climate is the right country for a new home. Go and see for yourself. You will be convinced as thousands have been before you. Low round-trip rates to all points and return, and the amount paid is refunded to those who buy.

I am now prepared to sell round trip tickets to Nebraska and return. The General Office of the B. & M. R. R. is at Lincoln, the Capitol of the State. I will sell tickets from Grinnell to Lincoln and return for $12.75, and the fare is refunded to those who buy. Write to me or call for a circular and for full information or for tickets to Lincoln or other points.

E. R. Potter, Grinnell, Iowa

SWEDISH CONTRACT LABOR---1883

Contract labor among the Scandinavians was not a common practice. Occasionally, however, groups of Scandinavian contract laborers were imported to work in manufacturing establishments. The following selection describes one such group and their difficulties in a New Hampshire town. (Source: New York Times, July 4, 1883.)

The Swedish and Norwegian minister has called the attention of the Secretary of State of the United States to what are claimed by him to be several illegal arrests and imprisonments of Swedish immigrants by manufacturing corporations of Suncook. The companies have been importing help from these countries, and it is claimed by the corporations that the persons so imported owe the companies their passage money, which the operatives deny. The matter was referred by the United States Government to the Government of New Hampshire, which has placed the whole subject in the hands of the Hon. Mason W. Tappan, Attorney General, who will investigate the matter and report thereon.

Through some of their countrymen, the arrested immigrants have sent a petition to the Swedish Minister at Washington setting forth that far away from their homes, in a new country, whose language they cannot speak, and whose laws they do not understand, they have on charges unknown to them been arrested and imprisoned, and asking that they be released, and be allowed damages for false incarceration. The arresting officer says, however, that in every case an interpreter was furnished, and the accused men were told that the charges were for debt, and the arrests were made in the belief that they were about to leave the state. Of the 165 Swedes the Suncook corporations have received through the Inman Steam-Ship Line, more than half have gone away, leaving tradespeople their creditors to the amount of $1,000. It is stated that the corporations contracted for trustworthy help, but that many of the Swedes are unreliable, there being a number of insane persons, idiots, and jailbirds among them. The Swedish Minister was informed that the operatives were arrested and imprisoned on account of not paying their passage money. advanced by the corporations, but this statement may not be true.

131

This selection vividly describes the loneliness, isolation, and monotony of life on the prairie farms of the Dakotas and Nebraska, which the
author claims accounts for the high percentage of insanity among Scandinavians in those regions. This description, and others like it, are
echoed even more dramatically in the classic novel by Ole Edvart Rolvaag,
Giants in the Earth.
(Source: E. V. Smalley, "The Isolation of Life on Prairie Farms," Atlantic Monthly, 1893.)

. . . . In no civilized country have the cultivators of the soil adapted
their home life so badly to the conditions of nature as have the people of
our great Northwestern prairies. This is a strong statement, but I am
led to the conclusion by ten years of observation in our plains region.
The European farmer lives in a village, where considerable social enjoyment is possible. The women gossip at the village well, and visit frequently at one another's houses; the children find playmates close at hand;
there is a school, and, if the village be not a very small one, a church.
The post wagon, with its uniformed postilion merrily blowing his horn,
rattles through the street every day, and makes an event that draws people
to the doors and windows. The old men gather of summer evenings to
smoke their pipes and talk of the crops; the young men pitch quoits and
play ball on the village green. Now and then a detachment of soldiers
from some garrison town halts to rest. A peddler makes his rounds.
A black-frocked priest tarries to join in the chat of the elder people, and to
ask after the health of the children. In a word, something takes place to
break the monotony of daily life. The dwellings, if small and meagerly
furnished, have thick walls of brick or stone that keep out the summer's
heat and the winter's chill.
Now contrast this life of the European peasant, to which there is a
joyous side that lightens labor and privation, with the life of a poor settler
on a homestead claim in one of the Dakotas or Nebraska. Every home-
steader must live upon his claim for five years to perfect his title and get
his patent; so that if there were not the universal American custom of isolated farm life to stand in the way, no farm villages would be possible in
the first occupancy of a new region in the West without a change in our
land laws. If   the country were so thickly settled that every quarter-
section of land (160 acres) had a family upon it, each family would be half
a mile from any neighbor, supposing the houses to stand in the centre of
the farms, and in any case the average distance between them could not be
less. But many settlers own 320 acres, and a few have a square mile of
land, 640 acres. Then there are school sections, belonging to the State,
and not occupied at all, and everywhere you find vacant tracts owned by
Eastern speculators or by mortgage companies, to which former settlers
have abandoned their claims, going to newer regions, and leaving their
debts and their land behind. Thus the average space separating the farm-
steads is, in fact, always more than half a mile, and many settlers must go
a mile or two to reach a neighbor's house. This condition obtains not on
the frontiers alone, but in fairly well peopled agricultural districts.

If there be any region in the world where the natural gregarious instincts of mankind should assert itself, that region is our Northwestern prairies, where a short hot summer is followed by a long cold winter, and where there is little in the aspect of nature to furnish food for thought. On every hand the treeless plain stretches away to the horizon line. In summer, it is checkered with grain fields or carpeted with grass and flowers, and it is inspiring in its color and vastness; but one mile of it is almost exactly like another, save where some watercourse nurtures a fringe of willows and cottonwoods. When the snow covers the ground the prospect is bleak and dispiriting. No brooks babble under icy armor. There is no bird life after the wild geese and ducks have passed on their way south. The silence of death rests on the vast landscape, save when it is swept by cruel winds that search out every chink and cranny of the buildings, and drive through each unguarded aperture the dry, powdery snow. In such a region, you would expect the dwellings to be of substantial construction, but they are not. The new settler is too poor to build of brick or stone. He hauls a few loads of lumber from the nearest railway station, and puts up a frail little house of two, three or four rooms that looks as though the prairie winds would blow it away. Were it not for the invention of tarred building-paper, the flimsy walls would not keep out the wind and snow. With this paper the walls are sheathed under the weatherboards. The barn is often a nondescript affair of sod walls and straw roof. Lumber is much too dear to be used for dooryard fences, and there is no inclosure about the house. A barbed-wire fence surrounds the barnyard. Rarely are there any trees, for on the prairies trees grow very slowly, and must be nursed with care to get a start. There is a saying that you must first get the Indian out of the soil before a tree will grow at all; which means that some savage quality must be taken from the ground by cultivation.

In this cramped abode, from the windows of which there is nothing more cheerful in sight than the distant houses of other settlers, just as ugly and lonely, and stacks of straw and unthreshed grain, the farmer's family must live. In the summer there is a school for the children, one, two, or three miles away; but in the winter the distances across the snow-covered plains are too great for them to travel in severe weather; the schoolhouse is closed, and there is nothing for them to do but to house themselves and long for spring. Each family must live mainly to itself, and life, shut up in the little wooden farmhouses, cannot well be very cheerful. A drive to the nearest town is almost the only diversion. There the farmers and their wives gather in the stores and manage to enjoy a little sociability. The big coal stove gives out a grateful warmth, and there is a pleasant odor of dried codfish, groceries, and readymade clothing. The women look at the display of thick cloths and garments, and wish the crop had been better, so that they could buy some of the things of which they are badly in need. The men smoke corncob pipes and talk politics. It is a cold drive home across the wind-swept prairies, but at least they have had a glimpse of a little broader and more comfortable life than that of the isolated farm.

There are few social events in the life of these prairie farmers to enliven the monotony of the long winter evenings; no singing schools, spelling-schools, debating clubs, or church gatherings. Neighborly calls are infrequent, because of the long distances which separate the farmhouses, and because, too, of the lack of homogeneity of the people. They have no common past to talk about. They were strangers to one another when they arrived in this new land, and their work and ways have not thrown them much together. Often the strangeness is intensified by the differences of national origin. There are Swedes, Norwegians, Germans, French Canadians, and perhaps even such peculiar people as Finns and Icelanders, among the settlers, and the Americans come from many different States. It is hard to establish any social bond in such a mixed population, yet one and all need social intercourse, as the thing most essential to pleasant living, after food, fuel, shelter, and clothing. An alarming amount of insanity occurs in the new prairie States among farmers and their wives. In proportion to their numbers, the Scandinavian settlers furnish the largest contingent to the asylums.

The reason is not far to seek. These people came from cheery little farm villages. Life in the fatherland was hard and toilsome, but it was not lonesome. Think for a moment how great the change must be from the white-walled, red-roofed village of a Norway fiord, with its church and schoolhouse, its fishing-boats on the blue inlet, and its green mountain walls towering aloft to snow fields, to an isolated cabin on a Dakota prairie, and say if it is any wonder that so many Scandinavians lose their mental balance . . . .

THE LONE EAGLE---1927

One of the most famous of all Scandinavian-Americans is Charles Lindbergh, the son of Swedish immigrants. In the Spring of 1927, Lindbergh accomplished what no man had ever done before----he flew non-stop across the Atlantic to Paris in a single engine airplane. This selection is a portion of an article about Lindbergh's life that appeared in a New York newspaper.

(Source: New York Times, May 21, 1927.)

St. Louis. May 20.---From his mother, who journeyed from Detroit to New York to wish her son God-speed, to the most cynical aviation expert, all those who know Charlie Lindbergh believe that if the New York to Paris flight can be made by one man, he will do it.

He is expected to emulate his legendary ancestors, the Vikings, of daring exploits and intrepid venture. More than six feet tall, Lindbergh is slim (he is often called "Slim") and handsome, with an eagerness and freshness that goes with a man who does things. He is 25 years old. His fair hair and blue eyes give token of his Viking ancestry.

His Early School Days.

Lindbergh was born in Detroit in 1902, but the family home has been in Little Falls, Minn. since 1886. His mother, Mrs. Evangeline Lindbergh, lives in Detroit, where she teaches chemistry in the Technical High School. His two stepsisters have married and moved away from Little Falls. His father, the late Charles A. Lindbergh, was in Congress from 1906 to 1916.

Lindbergh was graduated from Little Falls High School in 1918 at the age of 16 and took a year of chemical engineering at the University of Wisconsin.

Then he returned to the family home and tilled the soil while his father was engaged in politics. When he was not behind the plow or harvesting the youth was driving a motorcycle or an automobile at a hairraising rate, almost invariably alone.

Takes Up Aircraft.

It was in 1921 that Lindbergh shook the mud from the fields off his shoes, climbed on his motorcycle and chugged to Lincoln, Nebraska, where he entered the Lincoln Standard Aircraft Company's flying school. There he thrilled the pilots and mechanics with stunts on his motorcycle and got his first flying experience.

He is remembered there for the insatiable interest he displayed in everything that could get off the ground into the air. Whenever a new model plane, or one with which he was not familiar, landed at the field he inspected it with great curiosity and asked questions about everything he did not understand . . . .

Then he decided to enroll for the army course. So he got on his motorcycle and rode to Kelly Field at San Antonio, Texas.

For two years "Lindy," as he was known at Kelly Field, studied under the army instructors and reveled in the daily excitement of flying the great assortment of training planes. He also acquired the knowledge of navigation, which gives him the confidence to start for Paris depending solely on his own navigating ability.

After a year in the Army Flying Service following his schooling at Kelly Field, Lindbergh went to Lambert-St. Louis Field, near St. Louis, in October, 1925, to go to work for the Robertson Aircraft Company. He was riding his coughing motorcycle. He did a few hair-raising ground stunts on the field and that was his introduction.

When "Slim," as he continued to be called at the St. Louis field, arrived he was a First Lieutenant in the Army Air Reserve. He joined the Missouri National Guard, Thirty-fifth Division, Air Corps, and by December of 1925 he was a Captain in the reserve and the National Guard and flight commander of the 110th Observation Squadron.

Begins Air Mail Flying.

He began flying air mail planes to Chicago and back for the Robertson Aircraft Company in April, 1923. Four times something happened to the engine of the De Haviland plane he was flying and he leaped over the side of the plane in the night as the ship plunged, nose downward, toward the earth. Four times his parachute worked and he automatically became a member of the Caterpillar Club, an exclusive organization of aviators who have saved their lives by a parachute leap.

All this time his ambition to make the New York to Paris hop was gaining strength, and finally he obtained the backing of the St. Louis group, which has unshakable faith that he can do it. Having tested out the plane made especially for his flight, the "Spirit of St. Louis," he sat down in its cockpit late one afternoon in San Diego and got out of it the next morning in St. Louis, having made a hop of 1,600 miles without stop in a little over fourteen hours and having established a new record for a one man, long distance flight . . . .

ROCKNE OF NOTRE DAME---1931

Probably the greatest Norwegian-American figure of the 1920's was Notre Dame's unsurpassed football coach Knute Rockne, who had been born in Voss, Norway. In 1931, he was killed in an airplane crash. The tributes paid to Rockne's memory exceeded anything known in the history of athletics. What follows is a portion of his obituary.
(Source: New York Times, March 31, 1931.)

NATIVE OF NORWAY.

When Knute Rockne first went to Notre Dame as a freshman in 1910, he explained later, he was "looking only for an education--to my mind, college players were supermen to whose heights I could never aspire."

He had been about six years getting to the college at South Bend, Indiana, after he was graduated from the Northwestern Division High School (now Tully) in Chicago. He had to earn the money first. By working as a railroad brakeman and later as a mail clerk in Chicago he accumulated $1,000 and reached the age of 22.

His original intention was to go to the University of Illinois when he had saved this much, but two of his friends were going to Notre Dame at the time and they urged him to go with them. According to his own explanation of his decision, the chief inducement was the possibility of living more cheaply at South Bend.

Since his father brought him to this country at the age of 6 from Voss, Norway, where he was born, the cost of living was the chief thing that affected Knute Rockne's life.

Notre Dame made him a chemist, good enough to be an instructor during his last undergraduate year, and it also made him an end and captain of the football team who made forward-passing history in the combination of Dorais to Rockne on the plains of West Point.

After he was graduated from Notre Dame in 1914, Rockne returned there that Fall as assistant football coach. He became head coach in the Fall, 1918, succeeding Jesse C. Harper.

His tenure at South Bend was uncertain only once, in 1925, when J. R. Knapp, chairman of the Columbia football committee, obtained his agreement to come to New York if a release could be secured from Notre Dame on a ten-year contract which Rockne had signed the previous year. His salary would have gone from $10,000 a year to $25,000.

Premature publicity disturbed the negotiations, and Rockne traveled back from New York to South Bend, wondering publicly if he still had a job. In testimonial of the undiminished esteem of Notre Dame, a group of alumni in Chicago collected $2,000 and bought him a new automobile.

Rockne was born in 1889. He is survived by his wife, Bonnie Skiles Rockne of Kenton, Ohio, whom he married in 1914, and by their four children, William D., Knute Jr., Mary Jean and John V. The two older boys have already begun to play midget football . . . .

AN HISTORIAN LOOKS AT SCANDINAVIAN IMMIGRATION---1921

In 1921, the open door policy of the United States toward foreign immigration came to a close with the passage of the Immigration Act of that year. The distinquished historian, Samuel P. Orth, writing a book on the history of American immigration at that time, concluded his study of Scandinavian immigrants with an interesting appraisal.
(Source: Samuel P. Orth, Our Foreigners, New Haven, Connecticut, 1921.)

It is the consensus of opinion among competent observers that these northern peoples have been the most useful of the recent great additions to the American race. They were particularly fitted by nature for the conquest of the great area which they have brought under subjugation. . . . Above all, the Scandinavian has never looked upon himself as an exile. From the first, he has considered himself an American . . . . Without brilliance, producing few leaders, the Norseman represents the rugged commonplace of American life, avoiding the catastrophes of a soaring ambition on the one hand and the pitfalls of a jaded temperamentalism on the other. Bent on self-improvement, he scrupulously patronized farmers' institutes, high schools, and extension courses, and listens with intelligent patience to lectures that would put an American audience to sleep. This son of the North has greatly buttressed every worthy American institution with the stern traditional virtues of the tiller of the soil. Strength he gives, if not grace, and that at a time when all social institutions are being shaken to their foundations.

BIBLIOGRAPHICAL AIDS

This selective bibliography of Scandinavian immigration mentions only a small fraction on the relatively vast body of writing on the subject. I have listed only the works which I have found most useful, and those which constitute a basic starting point for the student interested in pursuing this field of study further. For convenience sake, the bibliography is divided into three sections; one section for each of the major Scandinavian groups----the Danes, the Norwegians and the Swedes. In addition, with the exception of the Danish bibliography, the various works are divided according to subject categories. Unfortunately, there are relatively few new works on Scandinavian immigration, and as a result, most of the materials cited are old, but valuable. However, several new monographs are also listed, and it is hoped that scholars will begin to reappraise this fruitful field of American immigration history in the near future. One further note concerning the bibliography on Danish immigration must be mentioned. Very few books have been written about the Danish immigrant in the United States. Source material for the history of the Danes that settled in this country must be found in the files of newspapers or official publications of societies or organizations. These, together with many pamphlets and unpublished materials, letters, and documents are now collected in the Dan-American Archives, Sohngaardsholm, Alsborg, Denmark, established in 1829, and the material is now available to students. Some facets of Danish immigration can also be culled from bibliographies concerned with the Norwegian-Americans, and Swedish-Americans. Finally, one should understand that, at the present time, there is no satisfactory general account of Scandinavian immigration to the United States.

A. DANISH-AMERICANS GENERAL WORKS

Bille, J. H., "A History of the Danes in America," Transactions of the Wisconsin Academy of Science, Arts and Letters, Vol. XI. Madison, Wisconsin, 1896.

Einar, Moses. Dania Society of Chicago. Chicago, 1962.

Jensen, C. C. An American Saga. Boston, 1927. This work depicts the struggle of a Danish immigrant to overcome his handicaps.

Lloyd, D. "Askov, A Study of a Rural Colony of Danes in Minnesota," in Brunner, E., Immigrant Farmers and their Children. New York, 1929.

Mortensen, Enok. Seventy-Five Years at Danebod. Tyler, Minnesota, 1961.

Nielsen, T. M. How a Dane Became an American. Cedar Rapids, Iowa, 1935.

Nyholm, Paul C. A Study in Immigrant History: The Americanization of the Danish-Lutheran Churches of America. Dubuque, Iowa, 1963.

Riis, Jacob A. The Making of an American. New York, 1901. The autobiography of a well known Danish-American newspaperman, author, and social reformer.

Winther, S. K. Take All to Nebraska. New York, 1936. The story of the making of an American family out of Danish immigrants; dramatically forceful.

Scholarly Articles

Christensen, T. P. "A History of the Danes in Iowa," Studies in the Social Sciences. Vol X, No. 2. 1931.

------------------"Danish Settlements in Minnesota," Minnesota Magazine of History. Vol. VIII. 1927.

------------------"Danish Settlements in Wisconsin," Wisconsin Magazine of History. Vol. XII. 1928.

------------------"The Danes in South Dakota," Historical Connections. Vol. XIV. 1928.

Egan, M. F. "Denmark and the Danes," National Geographic Magazine. Vol. XLII. August, 1922.

Lorenzen, P. "Rebuild Festival: Fourth of July Celebration on Danish Ground," American-Scandinavian Review. Vol. XVIII. June, 1930.

B. NORWEGIAN-AMERICANS

In addition to the works cited below, the Publications of the Norwegian-American Historical Association, Northfield, Minnesota, are invaluable, but too numerous to mention in their entirety in this selective bibliography. Some of their published works, however, will be cited at random in the various subject categories. Articles from the Association's journals are listed as Studies and Records.

General Works

Anderson, Rasmus B. The First Chapter of Norwegian Immigration, 1821-1840, Its Causes and Results. Madison, Wisconsin, 1896.

Babcock, Kendric C. The Scandinavian Element in the United States. Urbana, Illinois, 1914.

Bergmann, Leola N. Americans From Norway, N. Y., 1950.

Blegen, Theodore C., ed. Land of their Choice, Minneapolis, Minnesota, 1955.

------------------Norwegian Migration to America, 1825-1860. Northfield, Minnesota, 1931.

------------------Norwegian Migration to America: The American Transition. Northfield, Minnesota, 1940.

Flom, George T. A History of Norwegian Immigration to the United States. Iowa City, Iowa, 1909.

Gjerset, Knut. History of the Norwegian People. New York, 1915.

Larson, Laurence M. The Changing West. Northfield, Minn., 1937.

Nelson, O. N. History of the Scandinavians and Successful Scandinavians in the United States. Minneapolis, 1893.

Norlie, Olaf M. History of the Norwegian People in America. Minneapolis, 1925.

Qualey, Carlton S. Norwegian Settlement in the United States. Northfield, Minnesota, 1938.

Early Norwegian Migrations

Anderson, Rasmus B. America not Discovered by Columbus. Chicago, 1874.

Evjen, John O. Scandinavian Immigrants in New York, 1630-1674. Minneapolis, 1916.

Gjerset, Knut, Norwegian Sailors in American Waters: A Study in the History of Maritime Activity on the Eastern Seaboard. Northfield, Minnesota, 1933.

Hardy, Gathorne G. M. The Norse Discoveries of America: The Wineland Sagas. Oxford, 1921.

Haugen, Einer. Voyages to Vinland: New York, 1942.

Hovgaard, William. Voyages of the Northmen to America. New York, 1914.

Koht, Halvdan. "First Scandinavian Settlers in America," The American Scandinavian Review. XXXII. 1942.

The Early Nineteenth Century

Blegen, Theodore C., ed. Ole Rynning's True Account of America. Minneapolis, 1926.

Cadbury, Henry J. "The Norwegian Quakers of 1825," Studies and Records. I. Northfield, Minnesota, 1926.

Comfort, William W. Stephen Grellet, 1773-1855. New York, 1942.

Johnsen, Arne Odd, ed. "Johannes Nordboe and Norwegian Immigration: An American Letter of 1837," Studies and Records. VIII. Northfield, Minnesota, 1930.

Rohne, J. Magnus. Norwegian American Lutheranism up to 1872. New York, 1926.

Veland, Andreas. Recollections of an Immigrant. New York, 1929.

Norwegian Migrations to the Mid-West

Bremer, Fredrika. The Homes of the New World: Impressions of America. New York, 1853.

Crofford, H. E. "Pioneer Days in North Dakota," North Dakota Historical Quarterly. I. 1936.

Herigstad, Omon B. "Norwegian Immigration," Collections of the State Historical Society of North Dakota. II. 1927.

Howard, Joseph K. Montana High, Wide, and Handsome. New Haven, 1943.

Jones, Louis T. The Quakers of Iowa. Iowa City, 1914.

Lindquist, Emory K. Smoky Valley People. Kansas, 1953.

Qualey, Carlton C. "Pioneer Norwegian Settlements, in Minnesota," Minnesota History Magazine. XV. 1931.

Schaefer, Joseph. A History of Agriculture in Wisconsin. Madison, Wisconsin, 1922.

------------------"Scandinavian Moravians in Wisconsin," Wisconsin Magazine of History. XXIV. 1940.

Smith, G. H. "Notes on the Distribution of the Foreign Born Scandinavians in Wisconsin in 1905," Wisconsin Magazine of History. XIV, 1931.

Swansen, H. Fred. "The Norse in Iowa to 1870," Doctoral Thesis. University of Iowa, 1936.

Prairie Society

Clausen, Clarence A. & Elviken, R., ed. A Chronicle of Ole Muskego: The Diary of Soren Bache, 1839-1847. Northfield, Minnesota, 1951.

Duus, Olaus F. The Letters of Olaus Fredrick Duus, Norwegian Pastor in Wisconsin, 1855-1858. Northfield, Minnesota, 1947.

Gates, Paul W. "The Campaign of the Illinois-Central Railroad for Norwegian and Swedish Immigrants," Studies and Records. VI. 1931.

Gjerset, Knut. "Account of the Norwegian Settlers of North America," Wisconsin Magazine of History. VIII. 1934.

Jorgenson, Theodore, & Solum, Nora O. Ole Edvart Rolvaag. New York, 1939.

Larson, Laurence M. The Log Book of a Young Immigrant. Northfield, Minnesota, 1939.

Ödegaard, Örnuly. "Emigration and Insanity: A Study of Mental Diseases Among the Norwegian-born Population of Minnesota," Acta Psychiatrica et Neurologica, Supplementum. IV. Copenhagen, 1932.

Osland, Birger. A Long Pull From Stavanger: The Reminiscences of a Norwegian Immigrant. Northfield, Minnesota, 1945.

Raaen, Aagot. Grass of the Earth: Immigrant Life in the Dakota Country. Northfield, Minnesota, 1950.

Rolvaag, O. E. Giants in the Earth. New York, 1927.

Sandro, Gustav O. The Immigrant's Trek: A Detailed Study of Lake Hendricks Colony, in Brookings County, South Dakota Territory, from 1873-1881. Sioux Falls, South Dakota, 1926.

Sevareid, Eric. Not so Wild a Dream. New York, 1946.

The Norwegian Press in America

Anderson, Arlow W. The Immigrant Takes His Stand: The Norwegian American Press and Public Affairs, 1847-1872. New York, 1953.

Barton, Albert O., "The Beginnings of the Norwegian Press in America," Proceedings of the Wisconsin Historical Society. 1916.

Blegen, Theodore C., "The Early Norwegian Press in America," Minnesota History Bulletin, III. 1936.

Hertsgaard, J. P. Early Community History: Kindred, North Dakota, 1870-1900. Northfield, Minnesota, 1949.

Norlie, O. M. Norwegian-American Papers 1847-1946. Northfield, Minnesota, 1946.

Rugland, Sigvart Luther. "The Norwegian Press of the Northwest, 1885-1900," Masters Thesis. University of Iowa, 1929.

Education and the Church

Annual Reports of the Evangelical Norwegian Lutheran Church. Minneapolis, 1948.

Bergmann, Leola N. Music Master of the Middle West: The Story of F. Melius Christiansen and the St. Olaf Choir. Mineapolis, 1944.

Benson, William C. High on Manitou, A History of St. Olaf College 1874-1949. Northfield, Minnesota, 1949.

Fonkalrud, Alfred O. The American Scandinavian. Minneapolis, 1915.

Hetle, Erik. Lars Wilhelm Boe: A Biography. Minneapolis, 1949.

Horn, Harcourt H. An English Colony in Iowa. Boston, 1931.

Larsen, Karen. Laur Larsen: Pioneer College President. Northfield Minnesota, 1936.

Mulder, William. Homeward to Zion: The Mormon Migration from Scandinavia. New York, 1957.

Nelson, E. Clifford, and Fevold, Eugene L. The Lutheran Church Among Norwegian-Americans. 2 vols. Minneapolis, 1960.

Paulson, Arthur S., and Bjork, Kenneth, "A School and Language Controversy in 1858; A Documentary Study," Studies and Records. X. 1931.

Norwegians in the Cities

Bjork, Kenneth. Saga in Steel and Concrete: Norwegian Engineers in America. Northfield, Minnesota, 1947.

Hansen, Carl G. O. History of the Sons of Norway, 1895-1945. Minneapolis, 1945.

-------------------"The Story of Marcus Thrane," Sons of Norway. Minneapolis, 1949.

Hansen, Maurice B., & Blessum, Norman. Brief History of Normendenes Songforening, Chicago, Ill. 1870-1945. Chicago, 1945.

Hovde, Brynjolf J., "Chicago as viewed by a Norwegian Immigrant in 1864," Studies and Records. III. 1929.

McWilliams, Carey, "Minneapolis: The Curious Twin," Common Ground. 1946.

Perry, George S. "Your Neighbors: The Offerdahls," Saturday Evening Post. October, 1948.

Rygg, A. N. Norwegians in New York, 1825-1925. Brooklyn, 1941.

Stine, T. O. Scandinavians on the Pacific, Puget Sound. Seattle, 1900.

Strand, A. E. A History of the Norwegians of Illinois. Chicago, 1905.

Outstanding Individuals

Obviously many more books and articles about the lives and contributions of outstanding Norwegian-Americans could have been included. What follows is a random sampling.

Anderson, Rasmus B. Life Story of Rasmus B. Anderson. Madison, Wisconsin, 1915.

Blankfort, Michael. The Big Yankee: The Life of Carlson of the Raiders. Boston, 1947.

Blegen, Theodore C. ed. The Civil War Letters of Colonel Hans Christian Heg. Northfield, Minnesota, 1936.

Dennis, Charle H. Victor Lawson: His Time and his Work. Chicago, 1935.

Drfman, Joseph. Thorstein Veblen and his America. New York, 1943.

Eads, George. "N. O. Nelson, Practical Cooperator, and the Great Work He is Accomplishing for Human Upliftment," Arena. XXXVI. 1915.

Furuseth, Andrew. Sons of Norway. Minneapolis, 1961.

Gjerset, Knut. Norwegian Sailors on the Great Lakes: A Study in the History of American Inland Transportation. Northfield, Minnesota, 1928.

McGrath, John S. & Delmont, J. J. Floyd Björnstjerne Olson, Minnesota's Greatest Liberal Governor. St. Paul, 1937.

Michelet, Maren. Glimpses from Agnes Mathilda Wergeland's Life. (privately printed, 1916).

Odland, M. W. The Life of Knute Nelson. Minneapolis, 1926.

Phillips, James W. The Ole Bardahl Story. Minneapolis, 1963.

Rockne, Bonnie Skiles, ed. The Autobiography of Knute Rockne. Indianapolis, 1931.

Solum, Nora O. O. E. Rolvääg: A Biography. New York, 1939.

Wilson, Netta: Alfred Owie: Dentistry's Militant Educator. Minneapolis, 1937.

Some Recent Publications

Of the three Scandinavian-American ethnic groups, the bibliography concerned with the Norwegians is the most voluminous. For this reason I have listed a selection of some of the more recent works in this field.

Books

Anderson, Arlow W. The Salt of the Earth: A History of Norwegian-Danish Methodism in America. Nashville, Tennessee, 1962.

Beck, Bennett A. Brief History of the Pioneers of the Cromwell, Minnesota Area. Cromwell, 1962.

Blegen, Theodore C. Minnesota: A History of the State. Minneapolis, 1963.

Bronsted, Johannes. The Vikings. Baltimore, 1960.

Friis, Erik J. The American-Scandinavian Foundation 1910-1960: A Brief History. New York, 1961.

Gara, Larry. A Short History of Wisconsin. Madison, Wisconsin, 1962.

Hauge, Alfred. Cleng Peerson: Hundevakt. Oslo, Norway, 1961.

Knaplund, Paul. Moorings Old and New: Entries in an Immigrant's Log. Madison, Wisconsin, 1963.

Nelson, David T. Luther College, 1861-1961. Decorah, Iowa, 1961.

Rosdail, J. Hart. The Sloopers: Their Ancestry and Posterity. Broadview, Illinois, 1961.

Articles

Bjork, Kenneth O. "A Covenant Folk, with Scandinavian Colorings." Norwegian-American Studies. 1962.

De Pillis, Mario S. "Cleng Peerson and the Communitarian Background of Norwegian Immigration." Norwegian-American Studies, 1962.

"Early Norse Settlements." Sons of Norway, August, 1961.

Eggan, B. R. "The Norwegian Language Camp." Vinland. September, 1963.

Folkedahl, Beulah. "Norwegians become Americans." Norwegian-American Studies, 1962.

Hamsun, Knut. "On the Prairie: A Sketch of the Red River Valley." Minnesota History. September, 1966.

Holbo, Paul S. "The Farmer-Labor Association: Minnesota's Party Within a Party." Minnesota History. September, 1963.

Johnson, Derwood. "Reiersen's Texas." Norwegian-American Studies, 1962.

Levorsen, Barbara. "Early Years in Dakota." Norwegian-American Studies, 1962.

Rosholt, Malcom. "A Pioneer Diary from Wisconsin." Norwegian-American Studies, 1962.

Schurmacher, Emile. "The Fabulous 'Snowshoe' Thompson." Pacific Coast Viking. January, 1963.

Skardal, Dorothy. "The Scandinavian Immigrant Writer in America." Norwegian-American Studies, 1962.

C. SWEDISH-AMERICANS

The bibliography of Swedes in America is a large and useful collection. However, as with all Scandinavian groups, much of the material is relatively old. Exceedingly few new works have been produced in recent years.

General Works

Ander, O. Fritiof. "Reflections on the Causes of Emigration from Sweden." Swedish Pioneer Historical Quarterly. October, 1962.

Dowie, James I. Prairie Grass Dividing. Rock Island, Illinois, 1959.

Dowie, James I., and Espelie, E. M. ed. The Swedish Immigrant Community in Transition: Essays in Honor of Dr. Conrad Borgendoff. Rock Island, Illinois, 1963.

Hedin, Nahoth, and Benson, Adolph. Americans From Sweden. New York, 1950.

Hallendorf, Carl, and Schuck, Joseph. History of Sweden. Stockholm, Sweden, 1938.

Janson, Florence E. The Background of Swedish Immigration, 1840-1930. Chicago, 1931.

Johnson, Amandus. Swedish Contributions to American National Life. New York, 1921.

Lindberg, John S. The Background of Swedish Emigration to the United States: An Economic and Sociological Study in the Dynamics of Migration, New York, 1930.

Stephenson, G. M. The Religious Aspects of Swedish Immigration. New York, 1932.

Thomas, D. S. Social and Economic Aspects of Swedish Population Movements, 1750-1933. New York, 1941.

Westman, Erik G. The Swedish Element in America. Chicago, 1931.

Swedes in Colonial and Early America

Benson, Adolph B. Sweden and the American Revolution. New York, 1947.

Evjin, John O. Scandinavian Immigrants in New York, 1630-1674. Minneapolis, 1916.

Fernow, B. ed. Documents Relating to the History of the Dutch and Swedish Settlements on the Delaware River. Albany, 1877.

Jameson, J. Franklin. "William Usselinx, Founder of the Dutch and Swedish West India Companys." Papers of the American Historical Association. III. New York, 1887.

Johnson, Amandus. The Instructions for Johan Printz, Governor of New Sweden. Philadelphia, 1930.

------------------. The Swedish Settlements on the Delaware, 1638-1664. 2 vols. New York, 1911.

Holm, Thomas Campanius. A Short Description of the Province of New Sweden. Philadelphia, 1834.

Keen, G. B. The Swedish Settlements on the Delaware, 1638-1664. Philadelphia, 1911.

Nelson, Jacob A. John Hanson and the Inseparable Union. Boston, 1939.

Paxon, Henry D. Where Pennsylvania History Began. Philadelphia, 1926.

Shurtleff, Harold. The Log Cabin Myth. Cambridge, Massachusetts, 1939.

Ward, Christopher. New Sweden on the Delaware. Philadelphia, 1938.

------------------The Dutch and Swedes on the Delaware, 1609-1664. Philadelphia, 1930.

Swedish Immigration in the Nineteenth Century

Benson, Adolph B. "John Lindmark, Versatile Swedish Immigrant in New York." Year Book, American Swedish Historical Foundation. Philadelphia, 1946.

Bercovici, Konrad. "Swedish and Norwegian Farmers," On the New Shores. Chapter XV. New York, 1925.

Bergen, A. Swedish Settlements in Central Kansas. Topeka, Kansas, 1910.

Bremer, Fredrika. Homes of the New World. New York, 1853.

Carlson, Eskil, and Quist, Oval. "Early Swedes in Iowa." American Swedish Monthly. New York, 1948.

Erdahl, Sivert. "Erik Janson and the Bishop Hill Colony." Illinois State Historical Society Journal. 1925.

Forsbeck, F. A. "New Upsala: The First Swedish Settlement in Wisconsin." Wisconsin Magazine of History. XIX. 1935-36.

Johnson, William A. "Methodism and the Swedish Immigrant: The Life of Olaf Gustaf Hedstrom." Yearbook, American Swedish Historical Foundation. Philadelphia, 1962.

Linder, Oliver A. "The Story of Illinois and the Swedish People within its Borders." in The Swedish Element in America, vol. I. Chicago, 1931.

Lindstrom, David E. "The Bishop Hill Settlement." Year Book, American Swedish Historical Foundation. Philadelphia, 1945.

Mikkelson, M. A. The Bishop Hill Colony. Baltimore, 1892.

Olson, Ernst W. History of the Swedes of Illinois. Chicago, 1909.

Olsson, Nils W. "The First Swedes in Chicago." American Swedish Monthly. New York, 1948.

Pihlblad, C. T. "The Kansas Swedes." Southwestern Social Science Quarterly. XIII. 1932.

Rosenquist, Carl M. "The Swedes of Texas." Yearbook, American Swedish Historical Foundation. Philadelphia, 1945.

Stephenson, George M. "Pioneering in Wisconsin a Century Ago." American Swedish Monthly. New York, 1941.

------------------The Religious Aspects of Swedish Immigration. Minneapolis, 1932.

Swedes in the Civil War

Church, William C. The Life of John Ericsson. New York, 1941.

Dahlgren, M. V. Memoirs of Admiral John A. Dahlgren. Boston, 1882.

Hokanson, Nels. Swedish Immigrants in Lincoln's Time. New York, 1942.

Ness, George T. "Swedish-Born Graduates of West Point." American Swedish Monthly. New York, 1946.

Olson, Ernst W. The Swedish Element in Illinois. Chicago, 1917.

Roe, Louis A. Battle of the Ironclads. New York, 1942.

The Mass Migration of the Swedes

Ahlstrom, L. J. John Alexis Edgren, Soldier, Educator, Author, Journalist. Chicago, 1938.

Alexis, Joseph. "Pioneers in Nebraska." American Swedish Monthly. New York, 1948.

Angstrom, Martha. "Swedish Immigrant Guidebooks in the Early 1850's." Year Book, American Swedish Historical Foundation. Philadelphia, 1947.

Backlund, J. O. Swedish Baptists in America. Chicago, 1933.

Benedict, Edith P. "Sweden in Fiction." American Swedish Monthly. New York, 1936.

Bergin, Alfred. The Swedish Settlements in Kansas. Rock Island, Illinois, 1909.

Capps, Finish H. From Isolationism to Involvement: The Swedish Immigrant Press in America 1914-1945. Chicago, 1966.

Cedarleaf, Wallace E. "A Noble Experiment." (New Sweden, Maine), In Swedish Element in America. vol. I Chicago, 1931.

Jenson, Andrew. "The Swedish People of Utah and in the Mormon Church". In The Swedish Element in America. vol. I. Chicago, 1931.

Lund, Doniver A. Gustavus Adolphus College: A Centennial History, 1862-1962. St. Peter, Minnesota, 1963.

Mattson, Hans. Reminiscences, The Story of An Immigrant. St. Paul, Minnesota, 1891.

Nelson, Helge. The Swedes and Swedish Settlements in North America. Lund, Sweden, 1943.

Nyvall, Carl J. Travel Memories From America: Among Swedish Pietists in America, 1875-1876. Sweden, 1890.

Olson, Adolph, & Olson, Virgil A. Seventy Five Years---------------- Bethel Theological Seminary. Chicago, 1946.

Strand, Algot E. A History of the Swedish Americans of Minnesota. 3 vols. Chicago, 1910.

Swanson, Roy. "Frontiersmen of Minnesota." American Swedish Monthly. New York, 1948.

Outstanding Individuals

As with the Norwegian Americans, many more books and articles about outstanding Swedish Americans could have been included. Space limitations have prevented the expansion of this list.

Creese, James. "Charles Augustus Lindbergh." American Scandinavian Review. New York, 1927.

Cunningham, R. M. "The Man Who Understands Your Stomach," (Anton J. Carlson). Saturday Evening Post. September 13, 1947.

Detzer, Karl. Carl Sandburg, A Study in Personality and Background. New York, 1941.

Ekblaw, W. Elmer. Our Viking Industrialists. Worcester, Massachusetts, 1946.

Haines, Dora B., and Lynn, J. The Lindberghs. New York, 1931.

Jarman, Rufus. "Governor Youngdahl and the Gamblers." Saturday Evening Post. December 3, 1947.

Keen, Gregory B. The Descendents of Göran Kyn of New Sweden. Philadelphia, 1913.

Larson, Cedric. "Map King of New York," (Andrew G. Hagstrom). American Swedish Monthly. New York, 1940.

Lafgren, Svante. "Some Swedish Business Pioneers in Washington." Yearbook, American Swedish Historical Foundation. Philadelphia, 1947.

Rogers, Meyric R. Carl Milles, An Interpretation of His Work. New Haven, 1940.

Stephenson, George M. John Lind of Minnesota. Minneapolis, 1935.

Swanson, Roy W. "Mike Holm, Ten Times, Minnesota's Secretary of State." American Swedish Monthly, New York, 1940.

Swenson, Edgar. "Gustavus A. Eisen, Scholar and Benefactor." American Swedish Monthly. New York, 1935.

Wagenknecht, Edward. Jenny Lind. Boston, 1931.

INDEX